Breakfast
&
Brunch

Blueberry & Cream Cheese Strata

Kathy Grashoff
Fort Wayne, IN

This berry-filled strata is just right for a leisurely breakfast with family & friends.

16-oz. loaf white bread, crusts removed, cubed and divided
2 c. frozen blueberries, divided
3-oz. pkg. cream cheese, cut into 1/4-inch cubes
4 eggs
2 c. milk
1/3 c. sugar
1 t. vanilla extract
1/4 t. salt
1/4 t. nutmeg

Place half of the bread in a greased 8"x8" baking pan; top with half of the blueberries. Top with cream cheese, remaining bread and remaining blueberries; set aside. Beat eggs, milk, sugar, vanilla, salt and nutmeg with an electric mixer on medium speed until blended. Pour over bread mixture and refrigerate for 20 minutes to overnight. Bake, uncovered, at 325 degrees for one hour. Serves 4 to 6.

Serving herbal tea with breakfast? Drop a few sprigs of mint or several chamomile petals into the tea canister for a sweeter flavor.

Goose berry Patch Co.
Best-Ever Casseroles
CASSEROLES
Mom's Green Bean Bake
2 10-3/4 oz. cans cream of mushroom soup
1 c. milk
1 T. soy sauce
1 clove garlic, minced
pepper to taste
1 lb. ground sausage, browned and drained
2 16-oz. pkgs. frozen cut green beans
2.8-oz. can French fried onions, divided

A Country Store In Your Mailbox®

Gooseberry Patch
600 London Road
P.O. Box 190
Delaware, OH 43015

www.gooseberrypatch.com
1·800·854·6673

 1-931890-75-7
Fifth Printing, January, 2007

Do you have a tried & true recipe...
tip, craft or memory that you'd like to see featured in a **Gooseberry Patch** book? Visit our website at **www.gooseberrypatch.com**, register and follow the easy steps to submit your favorite family recipe.
Or send them to us at:

Gooseberry Patch
Attn: Book Dept.
P.O. Box 190
Delaware, OH 43015

Don't forget to include the number of servings your recipe makes, plus your name, street address, phone number and e-mail address. If we select your recipe, your name will appear right along with it...and you'll receive a **FREE** copy of the book!

Contents

Dedication
To all of our friends
who love serving up
homestyle food
for family & friends!
Appreciation
For taking time to keep in
touch and share your
best...we thank you!

Breakfast & Brunch

Morning Delight

Jane White
Kountze, TX

So delicious and easy to make...no one can resist it!

2 8-oz. tubes refrigerated crescent rolls, divided
2 8-oz. pkgs. cream cheese, softened
1 egg
1 T. almond extract
1 c. sugar
Garnish: sugar, cinnamon to taste

Press one tube of crescent rolls into the bottom of a greased 13"x9" baking pan; seal seams. Set aside. Mix cream cheese, egg, extract and sugar in a bowl; spread over rolls in pan. Top with remaining crescent rolls; sprinkle to taste with sugar and cinnamon. Bake at 350 degrees for 20 to 25 minutes, or until golden. Serves 6 to 8.

Vintage-style salt shakers quickly become the prettiest little containers for dusting powdered sugar or cinnamon on breakfast treats.

Quiche-Me-Quick

Sandy Bernards
Valencia, CA

The name may make you smile, but the taste will have you coming back for more!

1/2 c. butter
1/2 c. all-purpose flour
6 eggs, beaten
1 c. milk
16-oz. pkg. Monterey Jack cheese, cubed
3-oz. pkg. cream cheese, softened
2 c. cottage cheese
1 t. baking powder
1 t. salt
1 t. sugar

Melt butter in a saucepan; add flour. Cook and stir until smooth; beat in the remaining ingredients. Stir until well blended; pour into a greased 13"x9" baking pan. Bake at 350 degrees for 45 minutes. Serves 10 to 12.

Keep juices icy cold for breakfast...it's easy! Fill old-fashioned milk bottles with orange, apple or grapefruit juice, then set them inside a galvanized bucket filled with crushed ice.

Breakfast & Brunch

Eggs Olé

Patti Suk
Rochester, MN

Set out plenty of sour cream and salsa for spooning on top...tasty!

3 4-oz. cans diced green chiles
16-oz. pkg. Monterey Jack Cheese, sliced
1 dozen eggs
2 c. sour cream
salt and pepper to taste

Spoon chiles into a greased 13"x9" baking pan; top with cheese. Set aside. Beat eggs and sour cream together; pour over cheese. Sprinkle with salt and pepper; bake at 375 degrees for 30 to 40 minutes. Serves 12.

Colorful, vintage-style oilcloth makes the best tablecloth...it wipes clean in a jiffy!

Cheese, Bacon & Potato Tart

Kristi Vandenham
Fillmore, CA

Try substituting pepper or maple-flavored bacon for a new twist.

1 T. butter
1 lb. bacon
1-1/2 lbs. potatoes, peeled, sliced and divided
1-1/4 c. shredded Cheddar cheese, divided
salt and pepper to taste

Spread butter in an 8" round baking pan; place bacon over butter, arranging in spoke-like fashion. Bring bacon up the sides and over the edge of the pan. Top with half the potatoes; sprinkle with half the cheese. Layer with remaining potatoes and cheese; top with salt and pepper. Fold ends of bacon slices across the top; bake at 400 degrees for about one hour or until potatoes are tender. Serves 8.

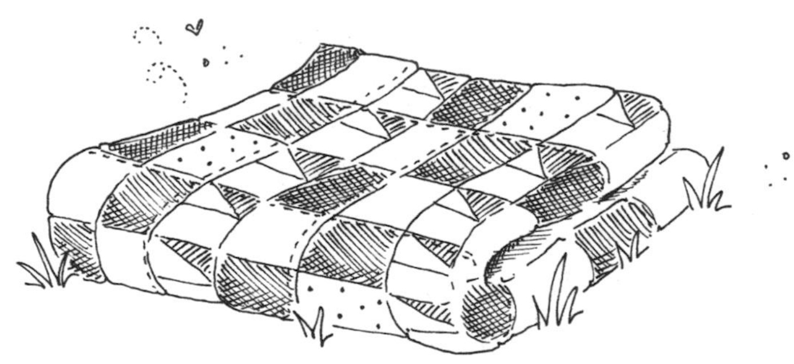

Take breakfast outdoors! Spread out a quilt on the picnic table and enjoy the cool morning air.

3-Cheese Western Omelet

Jane Skillin
Montclair, NJ

A classic omelet baked to cheesy perfection.

3/4 c. mild salsa
1 c. artichoke hearts, chopped
1/4 c. grated Parmesan cheese
1 c. shredded Monterey Jack cheese
1 c. shredded Cheddar cheese
6 eggs
1 c. sour cream

Spread salsa in the bottom of a greased 10" pie plate. Sprinkle artichokes over salsa; top with cheeses. Set aside. Blend eggs and sour cream together; spread over cheeses. Bake at 350 degrees for 30 minutes, or until set. Cut into wedges to serve. Makes 6 servings.

Wake up the family with a rise & shine omelet breakfast! Set out a variety of cheeses, vegetables and meats. Everyone can layer their favorite ingredients in a mini pie plate and get just what they want.

Rise & Shine Breakfast Soufflé

Lynda McCormick
Burkburnett, TX

A quick-to-fix overnight casserole.

1 lb. ground sausage, browned and drained
9 eggs
3-1/2 c. milk
1 t. mustard
6 to 8 slices bread, cubed
1-1/2 c. shredded Cheddar cheese
10-3/4 oz. can cream of mushroom soup
4 c. corn flake cereal, crushed
1/2 c. butter, melted

Mix sausage, eggs, milk, mustard, bread, cheese and soup in a bowl; spoon into a greased 13"x9" baking pan. Cover; refrigerate overnight. Remove from refrigerator 30 minutes before baking; set aside. Combine cereal and butter; sprinkle over egg mixture. Bake at 350 degrees for one hour. Serves 8 to 10.

Roomy, old-fashioned pop bottle carriers are just right for toting bottles of syrup or jars of jams & jellies to the breakfast table.

Breakfast & Brunch

Farmers' Favorite Casserole

Cindy Mosch
Green Bay, WI

This recipe is terrific when you substitute sausage and onion in place of the ham. I've also added green peppers and mushrooms to taste...just use your favorites!

8 frozen shredded hashbrown patties
4 c. shredded Cheddar cheese
1 lb. cooked ham, cubed
7 eggs
1 c. milk
1/2 t. dry mustard
1/2 t. salt

Arrange hashbrown patties in a single layer in a greased 13"x9" baking pan. Sprinkle with cheese and ham; set aside. Blend together eggs, milk, mustard and salt in a bowl; pour over ham. Cover and bake at 350 degrees for one hour. Uncover and bake an additional 15 minutes. Makes 8 servings.

Taking a breakfast casserole to an early-morning get-together? Wrap a pretty bandanna around the covered baking dish and slip the serving spoon inside the knot...keeps it right at your fingertips!

Pecan French Toast

Darcie Stearns
Rock Island, IL

This overnight, oven-baked French toast will win you raves!

1 loaf French bread, sliced
6 eggs
1-1/2 c. milk
1-1/2 c. half-and-half
1 t. vanilla extract
1/8 t. nutmeg
1 t. cinnamon

Arrange bread in a lightly greased 13"x9" baking pan; set aside. Beat together remaining ingredients; pour over bread. Cover; refrigerate overnight. Spread topping over mixture; bake at 350 degrees for 45 to 55 minutes. Let stand 5 minutes before serving. Serves 6 to 8.

Topping:

1/2 c. butter, softened
2 T. maple syrup
1 c. brown sugar, packed
1 c. chopped pecans

Mix all ingredients together.

Whip up tasty maple butter in no time...yummy on pancakes or French toast. Just combine 1/2 cup butter with 3/4 cup maple syrup.

Finnish Pancakes

Corinne Ficek
Normal, IL

A moist, custard-like treat that can be served with syrup, jelly or honey.

3 T. butter, melted
4 eggs
2 c. milk
1 c. all-purpose flour
1/8 t. salt
1 T. sugar
1 t. vanilla extract

Melt butter in a 13"x9" baking pan in the oven at 400 degrees; set aside. Place eggs in a blender; blend well. Add milk, flour, salt, sugar and vanilla; blend thoroughly. Pour into a pan; bake at 400 degrees for 35 minutes. Serves 4.

To add a splash of color to breakfast juices, freeze strawberry slices or blueberries in ice cubes. Toss several into glasses of juice right before serving.

Gold Rush Brunch

Kim McCorry
Rochester Hills, MI

Although the reason for the name remains a mystery, this hearty breakfast casserole will be an instant hit!

15-1/2 oz. pkg. frozen shredded hashbrowns with onions and peppers
1/4 c. butter
1/4 c. all-purpose flour
1/2 t. salt
1/8 t. pepper
2 c. milk
1 c. sour cream
2 T. fresh parsley, minced
8 slices Canadian bacon
8 eggs

Prepare hashbrowns according to package directions; set aside. Melt butter in a saucepan; blend in flour, salt and pepper. Stir in milk; cook until bubbly. Remove from heat; stir in sour cream, parsley and hashbrowns. Spoon into a greased 13"x9" baking pan; arrange bacon in the center. Bake at 350 degrees for 20 minutes; remove from oven. Make 8 depressions in mixture; place one egg in each. Bake for an additional 10 to 12 minutes. Serves 8.

When baking casseroles, remember that they'll cook faster in glass baking pans than they will in metal ones. It's simply because the heat can pass easily through glass.

Breakfast & Brunch

Creamy Crab Bake

Diana Chaney
Olathe, KS

An elegant breakfast casserole that is ideal for a bridal or Sunday brunch get-together.

2 eggs, beaten
2 c. milk
2 c. seasoned croutons
8-oz. pkg. shredded Cheddar cheese
1 T. dried, minced onion
1 T. dried parsley
1 lb. crabmeat
salt and pepper to taste
1/4 c. grated Parmesan cheese

Combine eggs, milk, croutons, Cheddar cheese, onion and parsley in a large bowl. Stir in crabmeat; sprinkle with salt and pepper. Spoon into a lightly greased 13"x9" baking pan; sprinkle with Parmesan cheese. Bake at 325 degrees for 45 to 55 minutes, or until a knife inserted into the center comes out clean. Serves 8.

Personalized votives are a snap to make. Cut a piece of parchment paper to fit around a votive holder. Write names on the parchment paper with a felt-tip pen. Simply wrap paper around votive and secure with double-sided tape.

Baked Apple Pancake

Kimberly Rocheleau
Ontario, Canada

Mmm, brown sugar, apples and cinnamon.

- 4 apples, cored, peeled and sliced
- 1/2 c. butter, softened and divided
- 1/2 c. brown sugar, packed
- 1 t. cinnamon
- 6 eggs
- 1 c. all-purpose flour
- 1 c. milk
- 3 T. sugar

Combine apples, 1/4 cup butter, brown sugar and cinnamon in a microwave-safe bowl; heat on high setting about 2 to 4 minutes, until tender. Spoon into a lightly greased 13"x9" baking pan and set aside. Combine eggs, flour, milk, sugar and remaining butter; blend until smooth and spread over apple mixture. Bake at 425 degrees for 25 minutes. Serves 6 to 8.

Old-fashioned salt & pepper shakers make the sweetest vases for tiny blooms. Just fill the shakers with water and slip the flower stems through the holes in the lids!

Amish Baked Oatmeal

Emily Nussbaum
Massillon, OH

Wonderful...there's nothing more to say!

1/4 c. butter, softened
1 egg, beaten
1/2 c. sugar
1 t. baking powder
1/2 t. salt
1/2 c. milk
1 t. vanilla cxtract
2 T. oil
1-3/4 c. quick-cooking oats, uncooked

Mix the first 8 ingredients together until smooth; pour into a greased 13"x9" baking pan. Stir in oats; bake at 350 degrees for 30 to 35 minutes. Serves 6 to 8.

Try something new...warm apple pie filling is delicious spooned over individual bowls of oatmeal.

Ham & Cheese Bake

Gloria Kaufmann
Orrville, OH

This is a favorite breakfast casserole for our family.

3 c. shredded Cheddar cheese
3 c. shredded mozzarella cheese
1/4 c. sliced mushrooms, drained
1/4 c. green onion, sliced
1/4 c. margarine
8-oz. pkg. cooked ham, diced
1/2 c. all-purpose flour
1-3/4 c. milk
8 eggs, beaten

Combine cheeses; sprinkle half in an ungreased 13"x9" baking pan. Set aside. Sauté mushrooms and onion in margarine until tender; arrange over cheese. Layer ham over the top; sprinkle with remaining cheeses. Set aside. Whisk flour, milk and eggs together; pour over cheese mixture. Bake at 350 degrees for 35 to 45 minutes; let stand 10 minutes before serving. Serves 10.

Make someone feel extra special...serve them breakfast in bed! Fill a tray with breakfast goodies, the morning paper and a bright blossom tucked into a vase.

Breakfast & Brunch

Southern-Style Spoonbread

Sharon Tillman
Hampton, VA

For Southerners, this is a "must-have" brunch dish.
Not one bite will be left!

3 c. milk
1-1/2 c. yellow cornmeal
1/2 c. butter, diced and softened
2 t. baking powder
5 eggs, separated
1 c. cooked country ham, diced

Bring milk to a slow boil in a large saucepan; gradually add cornmeal, stirring constantly. Reduce to low heat and cook, stirring constantly, for 10 minutes, until thickened. Remove from heat; add butter and baking powder and stir until butter is melted. Let cool and set aside. Beat egg yolks until light with a fork in a small bowl; stir into cooled cornmeal mixture. Add ham and mix until blended; set aside. Beat egg whites with an electric mixer on medium speed until stiff peaks form; fold into cornmeal mixture until well combined. Pour into a greased 2-quart casserole dish; bake at 350 degrees until a toothpick inserted in the center comes out clean, about 40 minutes.
Makes 6 to 8 servings.

Before filling a pitcher with syrup or honey, lightly coat it with oil. Then every bit of what's left will easily slip back into the original honey or syrup bottle.

Nutty French Toast Bake

Wendy Lee Paffenroth
Pine Island, NY

A great breakfast is in store when this is paired up with a side of fluffy scrambled eggs.

1 loaf French bread, torn into bite-size pieces
1 t. cinnamon
1 c. chopped nuts
1/2 c. raisins
6 eggs, beaten
1 t. vanilla extract
1 c. half-and-half
1 c. milk
1/2 c. maple syrup
1/2 c. brown sugar, packed
1/2 c. butter, melted

Mix bread, cinnamon, nuts and raisins together; spoon into a greased 13"x9" baking pan. Set aside. Beat eggs, vanilla, half-and-half and milk together; stir in maple syrup. Pour over bread; sprinkle with brown sugar. Drizzle with butter; refrigerate for at least one hour. Bake at 350 degrees for 45 minutes to one hour. Serves 6 to 8.

Plump raisins by covering them with boiling water and allowing them to sit for 15 minutes. Drain and pat dry with a paper towel before adding to a recipe.

French Toast Soufflé

Marybeth Biggins
Brockton, MA

I prepare this recipe for a "girls only" brunch that my friends and I take turns hosting once a month. It is so good!

10 c. bread, cubed
8-oz. pkg. cream cheese, softened
8 eggs
1-1/2 c. milk
2/3 c. half-and-half
1/2 c. maple syrup
1/2 t. vanilla extract
3/4 t. cinnamon
2 T. powdered sugar

Place bread in a greased 13"x9" baking pan; set aside. Beat cream cheese until smooth; add eggs. Mix well; stir in milk, half-and-half, maple syrup, vanilla and cinnamon. Blend until smooth; pour over bread. Bake at 375 degrees for 50 minutes; sprinkle with powdered sugar. Serves 6 to 8.

All happiness depends on a leisurely breakfast.
-John Gunther

Garden-Fresh Egg Casserole

Anne Muns
Scottsdale, AZ

Fresh tomatoes and spinach turn this breakfast casserole into something extra special. I think it's perfect for overnight guests.

1 c. buttermilk
1/2 c. onion, grated
1-1/2 c. shredded Monterey Jack cheese
1 c. cottage cheese
1 c. spinach, chopped
1 c. tomatoes, chopped
1/2 c. butter, melted
18 eggs, beaten

Mix all ingredients together; pour into a greased 13"x9" baking pan. Cover; refrigerate overnight. Bake at 350 degrees for 50 minutes to one hour. Serves 8 to 10.

Bacon curls make a tasty breakfast plate garnish. Just fry bacon until browned, but not crisp. Immediately roll slices and fasten each with a toothpick.

Georgian Cheese Grits

Jason Keller
Carrollton, GA

Light & fluffy...melts in your mouth.

6 c. water
1-1/2 c. quick-cooking grits, uncooked
3/4 c. butter
16-oz. pkg. pasteurized processed cheese spread, cubed
2 t. seasoned salt
1 T. Worcestershire sauce
1/2 t. hot pepper sauce
3 eggs, beaten

Bring water to a boil in a medium saucepan; stir in grits. Reduce heat to low; cover and cook for 5 to 6 minutes, stirring occasionally. Add butter, cheese, seasoned salt and sauces. Continue cooking and stirring for 5 minutes, until cheese is melted. Remove from heat; let cool slightly and fold in eggs. Pour into a lightly greased 13"x9" baking pan. Bake at 350 degrees for one hour, or until top is golden. Makes 12 servings.

It's easy to test eggs for freshness before adding them to a casserole recipe. Place eggs in a bowl or cup filled with water. If they float, it's time to replace them!

Fabulous Fruit & Nut Bake

April Jacobs
Loveland, CO

With almost everything but the kitchen sink in the ingredient list, you will find everyone asking for seconds.

1 lb. ground sausage, browned and drained
1-1/2 c. sugar
1-1/2 c. brown sugar, packed
2 eggs, beaten
3 c. all-purpose flour
1 t. baking powder
1 t. ground ginger
1 t. pumpkin pie spice
1 t. baking soda
1 c. coffee, chilled
1 c. raisins
3 c. boiling water
1 c. chopped walnuts

Crumble sausage into small pieces in a large bowl; stir in sugars until mixture is well blended. Add eggs and beat well; set aside. In a separate bowl, sift together flour, baking powder, ginger and pumpkin pie spice; set aside. Stir baking soda into cold coffee. Add flour mixture and coffee alternately to meat mixture, beating well after each addition. Combine raisins and water in a bowl; set aside for 5 to 10 minutes. Drain well; fold raisins and walnuts into cake batter. Turn batter into a well-greased Bundt® cake pan. Bake at 350 degrees for 1-1/2 hours, or until cake tests done. Cool in pan 15 minutes before turning out onto a serving platter. Serves 12.

Your favorite nuts, shelled or unshelled, will stay fresher longer if they're stored in the freezer. An added benefit, unshelled nuts will crack much easier when frozen!

Cheesy Chicken Brunch Bake

Kathy Grashoff
Fort Wayne, IN

Ideal for a Mothers' Day brunch or any time you're getting together with friends. Have plenty of fresh fruit to go alongside servings.

3 c. chicken broth
10-3/4 oz. can cream of chicken soup
9 slices bread, cubed
4 c. cooked chicken, cubed
1/2 c. instant rice, uncooked
1 c. shredded sharp Cheddar cheese, divided
2 T. fresh parsley, minced
1-1/2 t. salt
4 eggs, beaten

Combine broth with soup in a large bowl. Add bread and toss to coat. Add chicken, rice, 3/4 cup cheese, parsley and salt; mix well. Pour into a greased 13"x9" baking pan. Pour eggs over all and sprinkle with remaining cheese. Bake, uncovered, at 325 degrees for one hour. Serves 6 to 8.

Dress up mugs of chocolatey cocoa with scrumptious toppings like whipped cream and a dusting of cocoa, nutmeg, cinnamon or chocolate shavings. Breakfast becomes extra special!

Apple-Cinnamon French Toast

Lynda Purvis
Anchorage, AK

Yummy topped with warm maple, apricot, blueberry or raspberry syrup.

4 slices French bread, crusts removed, cubed and divided
8-oz. pkg. cream cheese, cubed
1 apple, cored, peeled and chopped
6 eggs
1 c. milk
1-1/2 t. cinnamon
2 to 3 T. powdered sugar

Place half of the bread into an ungreased 11"x7" baking pan. Top with cream cheese. Sprinkle with apple; top with remaining bread. Set aside. Beat eggs, milk and cinnamon together; pour over bread mixture. Bake at 375 degrees for 35 minutes or until set; sprinkle with powdered sugar. Serves 4 to 6.

A yummy topping for French toast...combine an 18-ounce jar of apricot jam with 1/2 cup orange juice in a saucepan. Bring to a boil and stir to blend; serve warm.

Breakfast & Brunch

Country Coffee Cake

Renee Spec
Crescent, PA

Whips up quickly and ready to enjoy in less than an hour.

1-1/2 c. sugar
3/4 c. butter
2 c. all-purpose flour
1 t. baking powder
2 eggs
3/4 c. milk
14-1/2 oz. can cherry or apple pie filling

Combine sugar, butter, flour and baking powder in a mixing bowl; mix well with an electric mixer on medium speed. Mixture will be crumbly; set aside one cup for topping. Beat together eggs and milk; stir into mixture in mixing bowl. Pour into a lightly greased 9"x9" baking pan. Spread pie filling over top; sprinkle with reserved topping. Bake at 350 degrees for 45 minutes, until golden. Makes 9 servings.

Breakfast treats are a great way to welcome newcomers to the neighborhood. Place the goodies in a basket and add teabags, coffee, jams & jellies. Don't forget to tuck in a list of suggestions for a favorite restaurant, repairman and vet.

Zesty Sausage Burritos

Joshua Logan
Corpus Christi, TX

Spice it up with hot sausage and Mexican-style Cheddar cheese.

2 lbs. ground sausage
1 dozen eggs, beaten
4-oz. can chopped green chiles
8 10-inch flour tortillas
8-oz. pkg. shredded Cheddar cheese
1 T. all-purpose flour
1 c. milk

Brown sausage in a skillet over a medium heat. Drain; reserve 2 tablespoons drippings in skillet and set sausage aside. Add eggs and chiles to skillet; cook and stir until eggs are done and set aside. Divide sausage, cheese and egg equally among tortillas. Roll up tortillas and place seam-side down in a lightly greased 13"x9" baking pan; set aside. Heat reserved drippings in skillet. Sprinkle with flour; stir. Add milk, stirring constantly, until mixture begins to thicken; pour over tortillas. Bake at 350 degrees for 10 to 15 minutes, until hot and bubbly. Serves 6.

To grate or shred a block of cheese easily, place the wrapped cheese in the freezer for 10 to 20 minutes...it will just glide across the grater!

Breakfast & Brunch

South-of-the-Border Enchiladas

Connie Hilty
Pearland, TX

Jazz up breakfast with these enchiladas...a new favorite!

1 T. oil
16-oz. pkg. frozen shredded hashbrowns
1 c. cooked ham, diced
4-1/2 oz. can diced green chiles
1-1/2 c. shredded Cheddar cheese, divided
28-oz. can green chile enchilada sauce, divided
8 10-inch flour tortillas

Heat oil in a skillet over medium-high heat. Add hashbrowns and ham; cook until golden. Stir in chiles and 1/2 cup cheese until cheese is melted. Spoon enough enchilada sauce into an ungreased 13"x9" baking pan to coat the bottom. Dip each tortilla in remaining sauce and fill with hashbrown mixturc. Roll cach tortilla as tightly as possible and place in baking pan seam-side down. Top with remaining sauce and cheese; cover with aluminum foil. Bake at 375 degrees for about 20 minutes. Remove aluminum foil and bake an additional 10 minutes, or until lightly golden. Serve immediately. Serves 8.

Make juice glasses sparkle! Dip the rims in water and roll in coarse sugar before filling with orange juice.

Goldenrod Bake

Jackie Smulski
Lyons, IL

This never-fail egg dish is delicious with a side of steamed asparagus. I often serve it as a springtime brunch.

2 T. butter
1/2 t. paprika
salt and pepper to taste
2 T. all-purpose flour
1 c. milk
3/4 c. shredded Cheddar cheese
4 to 6 eggs, hard-boiled, peeled and chopped
1/4 c. dry bread crumbs
1 t. fresh chives, snipped
bread triangles or English muffin halves, toasted

Melt butter in a saucepan; whisk in paprika, salt and pepper. Remove from heat; whisk in flour. Return to low heat; stir in milk, whisking continually until sauce thickens. Remove from heat; stir in cheese until melted. Add eggs; mix well. Pour mixture into a lightly greased 9"x9" baking pan sprayed with butter-flavored non-stick vegetable spray. Top with bread crumbs and chives. Bake at 350 degrees for 15 to 20 minutes, until bubbly. Spoon over toasted bread or English muffins. Serves 4 to 6.

Serving bacon with breakfast? Dip the strips into cold water before frying to keep the ends from curling up!

Breakfast & Brunch

Asparagus & Swiss Quiche

Nancy Likens
Wooster, OH

Ready in one hour...so quick, so tasty.

1 lb. asparagus, trimmed and cut into 1/2-inch pieces
2 8-inch pie crusts
1 egg white, beaten
10 slices bacon, crisply cooked and crumbled
2 c. shredded Swiss cheese
4 eggs
1-1/2 c. half-and-half
1/4 t. nutmeg
salt and pepper to taste

Place asparagus in a steamer over one inch of boiling water. Cover and steam until tender but still firm, 2 to 6 minutes. Drain and set aside. Place pie crusts into separate ungreased pie plates. Brush pie crusts with egg white; sprinklc with asparagus, bacon and cheese. Set aside. Blend together eggs, half-and-half, nutmeg, salt and pepper in a medium bowl; pour over cheese. Bake, uncovered, at 400 degrees for about 35 to 40 minutes, until firm. Let cool to room temperature before serving. Makes 2 quiches, 4 to 6 servings each.

A fresh breakfast side dish...fruit kabobs! Just slide pineapple chunks, apple slices, grapes, orange wedges and strawberries onto a wooden skewer. They can even be slipped into breakfast smoothies or frosty juices.

Strawberry-Walnut Breakfast Cake

Pat Habiger
Spearville, KS

If you like, another flavor of fruit preserves can be used...it always tastes great!

8-oz. pkg. cream cheese, softened
1/2 c. margarine, softened
3/4 c. sugar
1/4 c. milk
2 eggs, beaten
1 t. vanilla extract
2 c. all-purpose flour
1 t. baking powder
1/2 t. baking soda
1/4 t. salt
18-oz. jar strawberry preserves
1/2 c. chopped walnuts
1/2 c. brown sugar, packed

Combine cream cheese, margarine and sugar in a large bowl; beat until light and fluffy. Add milk, eggs and vanilla; mix well and set aside. Stir together flour, baking powder, baking soda and salt; add to cream cheese mixture and blend until smooth and batter is stiff. Spread half the batter evenly in a greased and floured 13"x9" baking pan; spread preserves over batter. Add remaining batter in dollops over preserves. Sprinkle with walnuts and brown sugar. Bake at 350 degrees for 40 minutes. Cut into squares; remove from pan while hot. Serve warm or let cool on a wire rack. Makes 12 servings.

Dip measuring cups and spoons into hot water before measuring butter...it will slide right out without sticking!

Cheese Blintz Casserole

Tori Willis
Champaign, IL

Super with warm jam or fresh berries spooned over each serving.

1-1/4 c. all-purpose flour
1 t. baking powder
3 T. sugar
1/2 c. plus 2 T. butter, softened and divided
3/4 c. milk
3 eggs, divided
16-oz. container cottage cheese
1 T. sour cream
1/2 t. salt

Combine flour, baking powder, sugar and 1/2 cup butter in a medium bowl. Mix well; stir in milk and 2 eggs. Set aside. Stir together cottage cheese, sour cream, salt, remaining butter and egg in a separate bowl; set aside. Spoon half the flour mixture into a lightly greased 9"x9" baking pan; top with cottage cheese mixture, then with remaining flour mixture. Bake at 350 degrees for 50 minutes, or until puffy and golden. Let cool slightly; cut into squares. Serves 6.

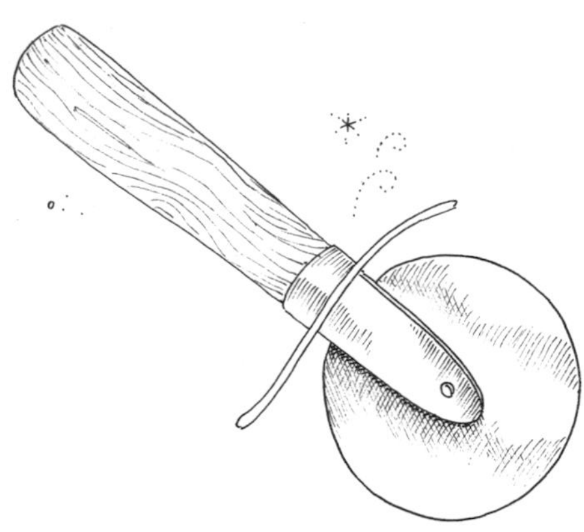

A pizza cutter makes quick work of dividing up casserole servings while the casserole is still in the baking pan!

Tangy Cranberry Breakfast Cake

Linda Hendrix
Moundville, MO

Three scrumptious layers!

2 c. all-purpose flour
1-1/3 c. sugar, divided
1-1/2 t. baking powder
1/2 t. baking soda
1/4 t. salt
2 eggs, divided
3/4 c. orange juice
1/4 c. butter, melted
2 t. vanilla extract, divided
2 c. cranberries, coarsely chopped
Optional: 1 T. orange zest
8-oz. pkg. cream cheese, softened

Combine flour, one cup sugar, baking powder and baking soda in a large bowl; mix well and set aside. Combine one egg, orange juice, butter and one teaspoon vanilla in a small bowl; mix well and stir into flour mixture until well combined. Fold in cranberries and zest, if using. Pour into a greased 9" round springform pan and set aside. Beat together cream cheese and remaining sugar in a small bowl until smooth. Add remaining egg and vanilla; mix well. Spread over batter; sprinkle with topping. Place pan on a baking sheet; bake at 350 degrees for 1-1/4 hours, until golden. Let cool on wire rack for 15 minutes before removing sides of springform pan. Serves 12.

Topping:

6 T. all-purpose flour
1/4 c. sugar
2 T. butter

Combine flour and sugar in a small bowl. Cut in butter with a fork until mixture resembles coarse crumbs.

Poultry

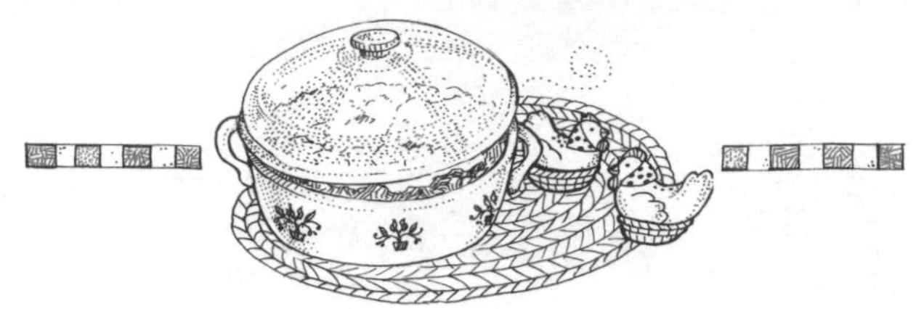

Quick & Easy Chicken Casserole

Jennifer Bean Bower
Winston-Salem, NC

Ready in only 30 minutes!

- 10-3/4 oz. can cream of chicken soup
- 10-3/4 oz. can cream of celery soup
- 2-1/2 c. water
- 6-oz. pkg. herb-flavored stuffing
- 3 10-oz. cans chicken, drained

Combine soups and water; stir until smooth and set aside. Sprinkle half of stuffing into a greased 13"x9" baking pan; top with half the chicken, then with half the soup mixture. Repeat layering. Bake at 375 degrees for 30 minutes, until bubbly and golden. Serves 6 to 8.

Chicken-Noodle Bake

Tracy Walters
Denver, PA

Cheesy with a nice, crispy topping.

- 12-oz. pkg. wide egg noodles, cooked
- 3/4 lb. pasteurized processed cheese spread, melted
- 2 boneless, skinless chicken breasts, cooked and cubed
- 2 10-3/4 oz. cans cream of chicken soup
- 1 c. chicken broth
- 1 c. dry bread crumbs
- 1/4 c. plus 2 T. butter, melted

Combine all ingredients except crumbs and butter in a large bowl. Mix well; pour into a greased 13"x9" baking pan and set aside. Combine bread crumbs and butter; mix well to coat and sprinkle over chicken mixture. Bake at 350 degrees for 30 to 40 minutes. Serves 6 to 8.

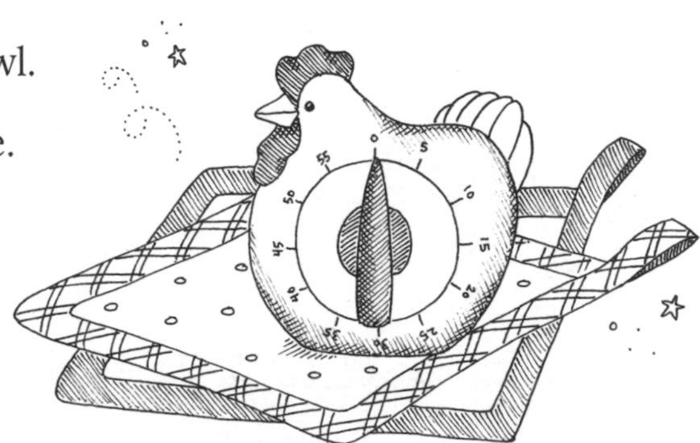

Turkey Tetrazzini

Shirley Gist
Zanesville, OH

Gobbles up leftovers...a must for the day after Thanksgiving!

8-oz. pkg. thin spaghetti, uncooked
2 cubes chicken bouillon
2 to 3 T. dried, minced onion
2 10-3/4 oz. cans cream of mushroom soup
8-oz. container sour cream
1/2 c. milk
salt and pepper to taste
2 c. cooked turkey, cubed
8-oz. can sliced mushrooms, drained
8-oz. pkg. shredded Cheddar cheese

Cook spaghetti according to package directions, adding bouillon and onion to cooking water. Drain and place in a large bowl. Stir together soup, sour cream, milk, salt and pepper in a medium bowl; fold in turkey and mushrooms. Lightly stir mixture into spaghetti, coating well. Pour into a lightly greased 13"x9" baking pan; top with cheese. Bake at 350 degrees for 30 to 40 minutes, until hot and bubbly. Makes 6 servings.

Whip up a gourmet salad in seconds! Purchase a bag of mixed salad greens and toss in fruit, nuts and grated cheese. Top off the salad with a drizzle of raspberry vinaigrette and toss.

Sour Cream Noodle Bake

Tami Bowman
Gooseberry Patch

To roast garlic, slice off the top of the bulb, making sure to cut the tips of the cloves. Place in a square of aluminum foil, drizzle with olive oil, wrap up and bake at 450 degrees for 25 to 30 minutes. Let cool enough to handle, then squeeze the cloves out of the skin.

1 lb. ground turkey
1 t. salt
1/4 t. pepper
1 bulb garlic, roasted
8-oz. can tomato sauce
1 c. cottage cheese
1 c. sour cream
1 c. fontina cheese, shredded
1 bunch green onions, chopped
8-oz. pkg. medium egg noodles, cooked
1 c. shredded Cheddar cheese

Brown turkey in a large skillet sprayed with non-stick vegetable spray; drain. Sprinkle with salt and pepper. Stir in garlic and tomato sauce; reduce heat and simmer for 5 minutes and set aside. In a medium bowl, combine cottage cheese, sour cream, fontina cheese and green onions; set aside. Spread half the turkey mixture in a lightly greased 2-quart casserole dish; top with half the noodles, then half the cheese mixture. Repeat layers. Sprinkle with Cheddar cheese and bake at 350 degrees for 20 minutes or until cheese is bubbly. Serves 4 to 6.

Serve a side of zesty herbed carrots...ready in only 15 minutes. Combine one pound of sliced carrots with 1/4 cup balsamic vinaigrette dressing and cook over medium heat for 10 minutes. Top with 2 tablespoons fresh parsley and 2 tablespoons chopped walnuts.

Homestyle Turkey & Rice Bake

Angela Murphey
Tempe, AZ

A snap to make and a nice change of pace from traditional-style cabbage rolls.

1 head cabbage, sliced into wedges
1 lb. ground turkey
1 onion, chopped
1/2 c. long-cooking rice, uncooked
salt and pepper to taste
10-3/4 oz. can tomato soup
1-1/4 c. water
14-1/2 oz. can stewed tomatoes

Place cabbage in a greased 13"x9" baking dish; set aside. Brown turkey and onion together over medium heat until turkey is no longer pink and onion is translucent; drain. Stir in rice, salt and pepper. Spoon turkey mixture over cabbage; set aside. Stir together tomato soup and water; add stewed tomatoes and pour over turkey. Cover and bake at 350 degrees for 30 to 45 minutes, until rice and cabbage are tender. Serves 4.

To cut down on casserole prep time, stock up on pre-cut and peeled veggies available in the grocery produce aisle or salad bar.

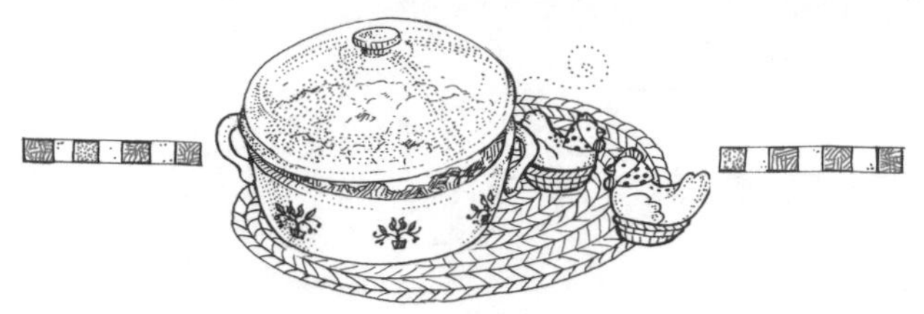

Jimmy's Greek Lemon Chicken

Kat Sadi
San Luis Obispo, CA

Dad was a great Greek cook in the Greek Navy. This recipe was one of his special Sunday night dinners.

16-oz. pkg. spaghetti, uncooked
2 T. dried oregano
2 T. dried basil
2 t. salt
1 t. pepper
2 lemons, divided
1/4 c. olive oil
5 cloves garlic, pressed
3 to 4-lb. roasting chicken

Boil spaghetti for 4 to 5 minutes, until bendable but not tender; set aside. Combine oregano, basil, salt and pepper, olive oil and garlic; rub over chicken. Pierce one lemon with a fork; place inside chicken cavity and place chicken in a roaster pan. Squeeze juice of remaining lemon; sprinkle over chicken. Add water to cover bottom of roaster. Bake at 350 degrees for 1-1/2 to 2 hours, basting and adding more water as needed, until juices run clear when pierced. Add spaghetti to roaster; return to oven for an additional 4 to 5 minutes, until pasta is tender. Slice chicken; serve with juices over pasta. Makes 6 to 8 servings.

The sweet, peppery flavor of basil goes with almost any dish, so keep some potted basil on your windowsill to snip any time of year!

Chicken Mozzarella

Mary Gildenpfennig
Harsens Island, MI

I like portabella mushrooms in this recipe and sometimes I substitute asiago cheese for a different flavor.

6 boneless, skinless chicken breasts
1/4 to 1/2 c. all-purpose flour
salt and pepper to taste
4 T. butter, divided
1/4 c. white wine or chicken broth
16-oz. pkg. sliced mushrooms
1/2 c. shredded mozzarella cheese

Pound chicken breasts to about 1/2-inch thick. Dredge in flour, salt and pepper, coating well. Melt 3 tablespoons butter over medium heat in a skillet. Add chicken; cook just until golden on both sides. Remove chicken to an ungreased 13"x9" baking pan. Add wine or broth and remaining butter to skillet; bring to a boil. Add mushrooms; reduce heat and simmer until soft. Top chicken with mushrooms; pour skillet drippings over mushrooms. Bake at 350 degrees for 45 minutes. Sprinkle chicken with cheese; bake for an additional 10 to 15 minutes, until cheese is melted. Makes 6 servings.

To get a crispy, crunchy casserole topping, don't cover the casserole dish while it's baking.

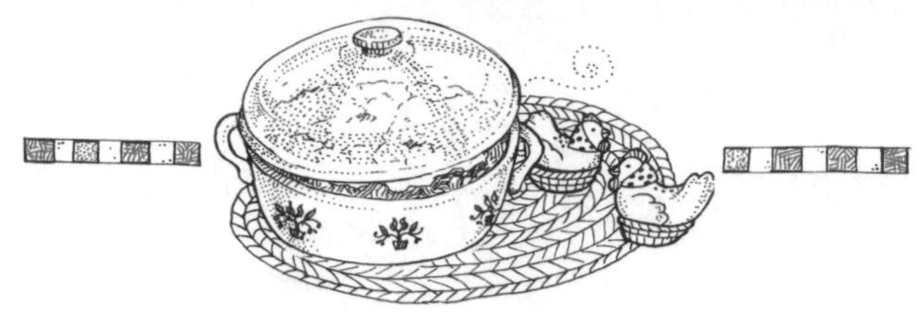

Turkey, Almond & Wild Rice Casserole

Shelley Turner
Boise, ID

The crunch of almonds and the tang of pimentos make this casserole oh-so delicious.

1 onion, chopped
2 T. butter
1/2 c. all-purpose flour
9-oz. can sliced mushrooms, drained and liquid reserved
3 c. half-and-half
1/2 to 1 c. chicken broth
2 c. prepared long-grain and wild rice
6 c. cooked turkey, cubed
1 c. slivered almonds, toasted
1/2 c. pimentos, diced
4 T. fresh parsley, chopped
salt and pepper to taste
1/4 c. butter, melted
1 c. dry bread crumbs

In a saucepan, sauté onion in butter over medium heat; remove from heat and stir in flour. Set aside. Combine reserved mushroom liquid with half-and-half and enough broth to make 4 cups. Gradually stir into flour mixture; cook and stir until thickened. Add rice, mushrooms, turkey, toasted almonds, pimentos, parsley, salt and pepper. Place in a lightly greased 13"x9" baking pan; set aside. Combine butter and bread crumbs; sprinkle over top of casserole. Bake at 350 degrees for 40 minutes. Serves 6 to 8.

Homemade chicken broth is simple to make. Whenever you boil chicken for a recipe, save the broth and freeze it. When it's time to make broth, thaw and combine with desired amount of chopped onion, chopped carrots and sliced celery. Simmer, uncovered, one hour and strain if desired.

Poultry

Herbed Chicken & Rice Bake

Jennie Gist
Gooseberry Patch

For a timesaver, put this together the night before and pop it in the oven the next day.

3 to 4 lbs. chicken
1 c. long-cooking rice, uncooked
2 10-3/4 oz. cans cream of chicken soup
1-1/4 c. water
1-1/2 oz. pkg. onion soup mix
1 t. dried thyme
1 t. Worcestershire sauce

Arrange chicken pieces in a lightly greased 13"x9" baking pan; set aside. Stir together remaining ingredients in a mixing bowl; spread evenly over chicken. Cover tightly with aluminum foil. Bake at 350 degrees for 2-1/2 hours, until rice is tender and chicken juices run clear when pierced. Serves 4 to 6.

I will see to it that no peasant in my kingdom will lack the means to have a chicken in the pot every Sunday.
-King Henri IV of France

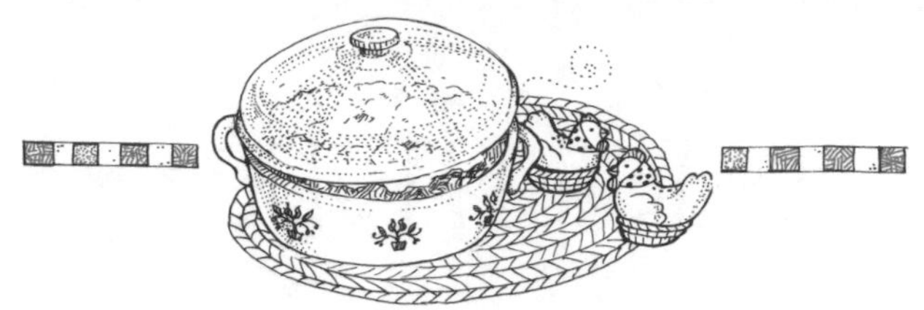

Balsamic Rosemary Chicken

Bobbi-Jo Thornton
Hancock, ME

The zing of balsamic vinegar really adds flavor.

4 boneless, skinless chicken breasts
2 T. Dijon mustard
salt and pepper to taste
2 T. garlic, minced
2 T. water
1/4 c. balsamic vinegar
4 sprigs fresh rosemary

Arrange chicken in an ungreased 11"x7" baking pan. Spread mustard over chicken; sprinkle with salt, pepper and garlic. Blend water and vinegar; sprinkle over chicken. Arrange one sprig of rosemary on each chicken breast; cover with aluminum foil and refrigerate for 2 to 3 hours. Bake, covered, at 350 degrees for 20 minutes; uncover and bake for an additional 10 minutes, until chicken is golden. Discard rosemary before serving. Makes 4 servings.

Turn any casserole into an au gratin. Simply sprinkle a prepared casserole with grated cheese and bread crumbs. Blend a little melted butter with dried herbs and drizzle over the casserole to moisten the bread.

Chicken Angelo

Jean Barris
Vermilion, OH

A very easy, simple dish to prepare...a must for any busy family.

4 boneless, skinless chicken breasts
2 eggs, beaten
1 c. Italian-style dry bread crumbs
1/4 c. butter, melted
8-oz. pkg. sliced mushrooms, divided
3/4 lb. sliced Muenster or mozzarella cheese
14-1/2 oz. can chicken broth

Dip chicken breasts in beaten egg; coat with bread crumbs and set aside. Heat butter in a skillet; sauté chicken just until golden on both sides. Arrange chicken in a lightly greased 13"x9" baking pan; top with half the mushrooms. Cover with cheese slices; top with remaining mushrooms. Pour broth over all. Bake, uncovered, at 350 degrees for 40 minutes, or until chicken juices run clear. Makes 4 servings.

Freeze homemade or extra canned broth in ice cube trays for terrific flavor when boiling rice. Ice cubes are also so handy when whipping up gravies or sauces for casseroles.

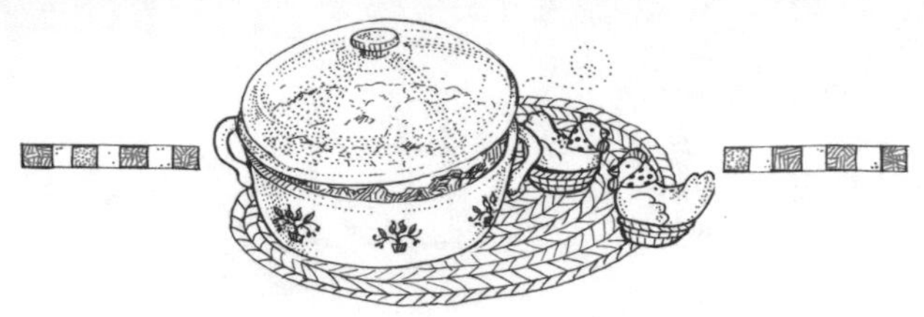

Cheesy Turkey Rellenos

Vickie

Try tossing in some jalapeños for a hotter version!

- 4 4-oz. cans whole green chiles, drained and rinsed
- 1/4 lb. Pepper Jack cheese, sliced into 1/2-inch strips
- 2 c. cooked turkey, sliced into 1/2-inch strips
- 1/2 c. all-purpose flour
- 1/2 t. baking powder
- 1/4 t. salt
- 1/2 c. milk
- 3 eggs
- 2/3 c. shredded Cheddar cheese

Slice chiles up one side; remove seeds and spread open flat. Arrange in a greased 11"x7" baking pan. Fill each chile half with Pepper Jack cheese and turkey strips. Fold chiles closed and place seam-side down in dish. In a medium bowl, combine flour, baking powder and salt. Whisk together milk and eggs; slowly add to flour mixture, beating until smooth. Pour over chiles. Bake at 450 degrees for 15 minutes. Remove from oven and turn off heat. Sprinkle Cheddar cheese over top and return to oven until cheese is melted. Serves 6.

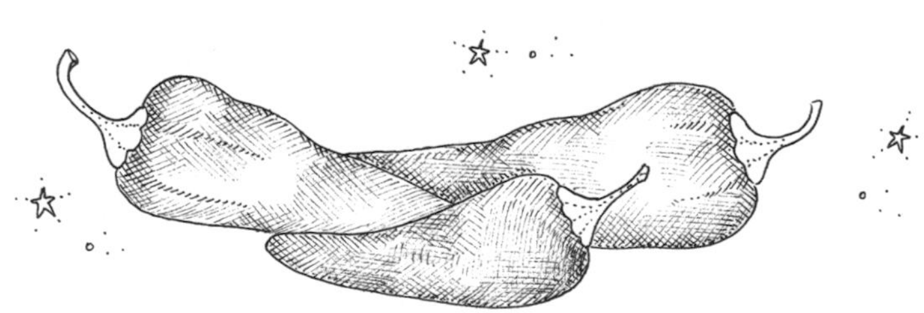

Unsure about the capacity of a baking pan...2 quarts or one? Just measure out one quart of water and pour into the pan to check.

Chicken Tex-Mex Bake

Jenny Flake
Gilbert, AZ

Simply stated...my family loves this dish!

2 12-1/2 oz. cans chicken, drained and shredded
2 10-oz. cans mild red enchilada sauce
10-3/4 oz. can cream of chicken soup
4-oz. can diced green chiles
14-1/2 oz. can diced tomatoes
2-1/2 c. shredded Mexican-blend cheese, divided
1 c. sour cream
1/2 c. onion, diced
1/2 t. pepper
10 flour tortillas, cut into 1-inch squares and divided
1/2 c. sliced black olives

Combine first 5 ingredients and half of the cheese; mix well. Blend in sour cream, onion and pepper; set aside. Arrange half the tortillas over the bottom of a 13"x9" baking pan sprayed with non-stick vegetable spray. Spoon a layer of chicken mixture over tortillas. Repeat layering, ending with chicken mixture on top. Sprinkle with remaining cheese; top with olives. Cover lightly with aluminum foil; bake at 350 degrees for 40 minutes, or until hot and bubbly. Serves 8.

Casseroles really taste better if they're made in advance to allow the flavors to blend. Make one the night before, then pop in the oven to bake the next day for dinner.

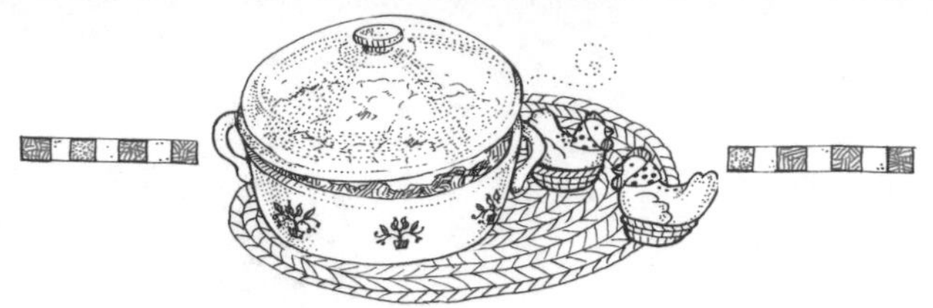

Zesty Turkey Tortillas

Megan Brooks
Antioch, TN

This casserole totes easily to any potluck or carry-in, and I never come home with leftovers.

1 T. oil, divided
1 onion, chopped
1 green pepper, chopped
1/2 t. salt, divided
1-1/4 c. sliced mushrooms
1-1/4 lbs. ground turkey
1 T. ground cumin
1 T. coriander
1 T. chili powder
28-oz. can stewed tomatoes
3 cloves garlic, minced
8 6-inch corn tortillas, divided
1 c. shredded Monterey Jack cheese, divided

Heat 1-1/2 teaspoons oil in a skillet over medium heat. Add onion, green pepper and 1/4 teaspoon salt; cook for 3 minutes, stirring occasionally. Add mushrooms and cook an additional 3 minutes; or until vegetables are tender. Add turkey and cook until no longer pink; drain. Stir in spices and remaining salt; cook, stirring constantly, for one minute. Stir in tomatoes and garlic; bring mixture to a simmer. Spread enough turkey mixture to cover the bottom of a greased 13"x9" baking dish. Cover with 4 tortillas; top with half of remaining turkey mixture. Sprinkle with half the cheese. Top with remaining tortillas, turkey mixture and cheese. Bake at 400 degrees for 25 minutes, or until bubbling and lightly golden. Serves 6 to 8.

Jazz up an ordinary casserole with something new…chile peppers, salsa, water chestnuts or baby corn.

Sour Cream-Chicken Enchiladas

Kim Turechek
Oklahoma City, OK

Keep extra sour cream, salsa, green onions and shredded cheese on hand for topping off each serving.

2 10-3/4 oz. cans cream of chicken soup
4-oz. can diced green chiles, drained
1/2 c. milk
1/2 t. ground cumin
1 c. sour cream
2 c. cooked chicken, cubed
3-oz. pkg. cream cheese, softened
1/4 c. onion, chopped
12 10-inch flour tortillas
1 c. Monterey Jack cheese, shredded

Combine the first 5 ingredients in a blender; blend until smooth. Set aside. Mix chicken, cream cheese and onion together; spread one to 2 tablespoons chicken mixture onto each tortilla. Roll up; place seam-side down in an ungreased 13"x9" baking pan. Top with sour cream mixture; sprinkle with cheese. Cover; bake at 350 degrees for 30 minutes. Uncover the last 5 minutes of baking. Makes 12 servings.

Keep sides a snap to make...toss coleslaw with Italian salad dressing or drizzle cucumber and onion slices with a sprinkle of balsamic vinegar. Crisp and delicious!

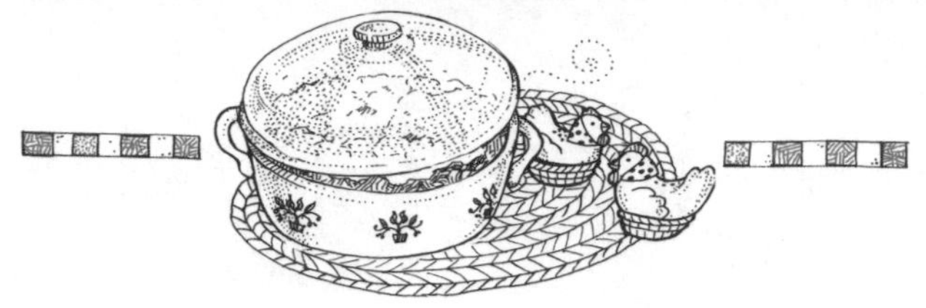

Turkey & Pasta Bake

Audrey Lett
Newark, DE

No one will complain about leftover turkey when you prepare this casserole. Always a winner!

6 c. prepared penne pasta
2 c. cooked turkey, cubed
2 c. plum tomatoes, coarsely chopped and drained
8-oz. container cottage cheese
1/2 c. shredded Cheddar cheese
4 green onions, sliced
1 t. dried basil
1/2 t. dried oregano
1/3 c. dry bread crumbs
2 T. dried parsley

Combine pasta, turkey and tomatoes. Spread in a greased 13"x9" baking dish; set aside. In a small bowl, combine cottage cheese, Cheddar cheese, onions, basil and oregano. Mix well. Spread over turkey mixture, smoothing with the back of the spoon. Toss bread crumbs with parsley and sprinkle over top. Bake at 350 degrees for 30 minutes. Serves 6.

Spend some extra time in the kitchen now to prepare and freeze several casserole dishes, then enjoy the rewards later when there's no time to cook!

Stuffed Pasta Shells

Holly Sutton
Middleburgh, NY

You'll have just enough time to make a crispy salad while this casserole is baking...it's ready in just 30 minutes.

1-1/2 c. chicken-flavored stuffing mix, prepared
2 c. cooked chicken, chopped
1/2 c. peas
1/2 c. mayonnaise
18 prepared jumbo pasta shells
10-3/4 oz. can cream of chicken soup
2/3 c. water

Combine stuffing, chicken, peas and mayonnaise; spoon into cooked pasta shells. Arrange shells in a greased 13"x9" baking pan. Mix soup and water; pour over shells. Cover and bake at 350 degrees for 30 minutes. Makes 6 to 8 servings.

To freeze a just-made casserole, let it sit at room temperature for 30 minutes, then refrigerate for 30 minutes more. When cool, wrap it tightly with heavy-duty aluminum foil; label and freeze up to 3 months.

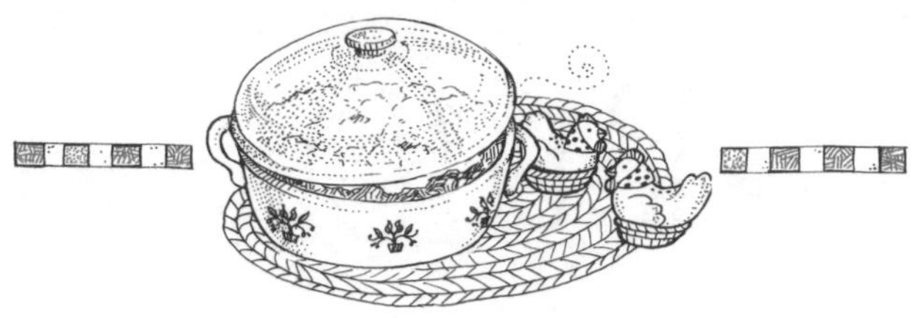

Swiss Chicken

Paula Lichiello
Forest, VA

This casserole can be prepared a day in advance...just refrigerate until you're ready to bake.

4 boneless, skinless chicken breasts, cooked and cubed
2 c. seasoned croutons
1/2 c. celery, sliced
1/4 c. onion, chopped
1/2 lb. Swiss cheese, cubed
1/4 c. sliced almonds
salt and pepper to taste
2 10-3/4 oz. cans cream of chicken soup
1/2 c. mayonnaise

Place chicken in a lightly greased 13"x9" baking pan. Sprinkle with croutons, celery, onion, cheese and almonds. Add salt and pepper to taste; set aside. Combine soup and mayonnaise. Mix thoroughly; pour over chicken mixture and spread evenly. Cover and bake at 325 degrees for 50 minutes. Uncover and bake an additional 10 minutes. Let stand 5 to 10 minutes before serving. Serves 6 to 8.

Need to thaw a frozen casserole? Up to 2 days before serving, set the frozen casserole in the refrigerator to slightly thaw. When ready to bake, cover loosely with aluminum foil and bake at 350 degrees for one hour. Remove aluminum foil and continue baking 20 to 30 minutes longer or until heated through.

Poultry

Broccoli-Chicken Lasagna

Monica Wilkinson
Burton, SC

A tasty twist on a familiar dish...the kids will love it!

- 1/4 c. butter
- 1/4 c. all-purpose flour
- 1 T. chicken bouillon granules
- pepper to taste
- 1/2 t. Italian seasoning
- 2 c. milk
- 2 c. shredded Italian-blend cheese
- 1 c. cooked chicken, diced
- 2 c. broccoli flowerets, cooked
- 4 strips prepared lasagna, divided

Melt butter in a saucepan over medium-low heat; stir in flour, bouillon, pepper and Italian seasoning. Gradually stir in milk; cook and stir until thickened. Add cheese; stir until melted. Mix in chicken and broccoli. Spread 1/2 cup mixture in the bottom of an 8"x8" baking pan sprayed with non-stick vegetable spray. Top with half the lasagna. Top with half the remaining sauce; repeat layers. Bake, uncovered, at 350 degrees for 30 to 40 minutes. Serves 4 to 6.

Turn ordinary silk flowers into something extraordinary! Clip their stems and add a little spray adhesive. Immediately sprinkle with extra-fine glitter and arrange several on a cake stand for a sparkly centerpiece.

Velvet Chicken

Katie French
Portland, TX

When I got married, my sister made a book of family recipes for me. This particular recipe was my sister-in-law's contribution to the book, and it is great.

6 to 8 boneless, skinless chicken breasts, cooked and cubed
10-3/4 oz. can cream of chicken soup
8-oz. container sour cream
1/2 c. margarine, melted
8-oz. pkg. pasteurized processed cheese spread, shredded
1 sleeve buttery round crackers, crushed

Combine chicken, soup and sour cream. Spread in a greased 13"x9" baking pan. Pour melted margarine over top; sprinkle with shredded cheese, then crushed crackers. Bake at 350 degrees for 20 minutes. Serves 6 to 8.

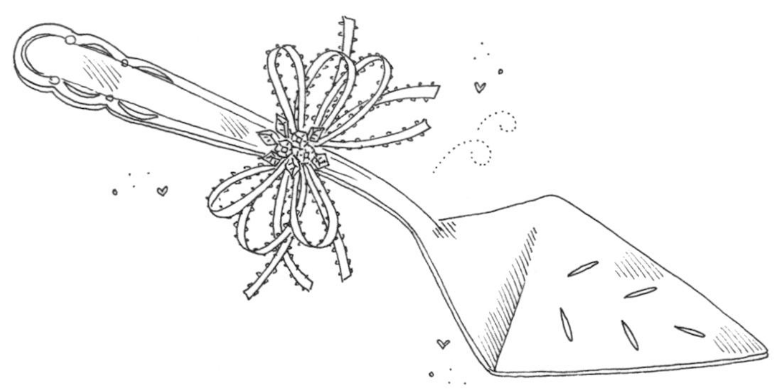

Just a dab of hot glue, some ribbon and vintage baubles can transform ordinary silverware into something extraordinary.

Famous Chicken Casserole

Heather Gibbs
Bonaire, GA

Other than the secret family recipe for our famous cheesecake, this is the most requested recipe I have. I recommend doubling the ingredients...everyone will want seconds!

- 10-3/4 oz. can cream of mushroom soup
- 10-3/4 oz. can cream of chicken soup
- 1 c. sour cream
- 1-1/2 lbs. boneless, skinless chicken breasts, cooked and cubed
- 2 c. buttery round crackers, crushed
- 4 T. butter, melted

Mix soups and sour cream together in a large bowl. Add chicken; stir until chicken is coated. Spoon mixture into a greased 8"x8" baking pan. Sprinkle with crackers, then with melted butter. Bake at 350 degrees for 30 minutes, until heated through. Serves 4 to 6.

Using paper cups? Then embellish them with surprises kids big and little will love! Faux jewels, stickers, wax seals and ribbon easily turn colorful paper cups from the party store into something special.

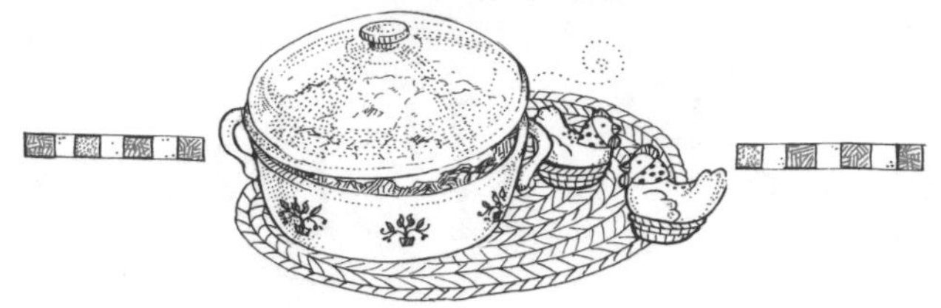

Oodles of Noodles Casserole

Beth Kramer
Port Saint Lucie, FL

To toast the almonds, just spread them on a baking dish and bake at 350 degrees for 10 to 15 minutes, stirring occasionally.

- 8-oz. pkg. medium egg noodles, uncooked
- 10-oz. pkg. frozen broccoli spears, cooked
- 2 T. butter
- 2 T. all-purpose flour
- 1 t. salt
- 1/4 t. pepper
- 2 c. milk
- 1 c. shredded Cheddar cheese
- 2 c. cooked turkey, diced
- 1/3 c. slivered almonds, toasted

Cook half the noodles according to package directions, reserving the rest for another recipe; drain and set aside. Melt butter in a saucepan over low heat; blend in flour, salt and pepper. Stir until smooth and bubbly. Gradually add milk, stirring until thickened. Remove from heat and add cheese; stir until melted. Dice broccoli stems, leaving the flowerets intact. In a lightly greased 8"x8" baking pan, arrange noodles, broccoli stems and turkey; pour cheese sauce over top. Lightly press flowerets into cheese layer; sprinkle with almonds. Bake at 350 degrees for 15 minutes. Serves 4.

Make dinner invitations fun! Gather pretty posies, tie on an invitation tag and deliver to your friends.

Poultry

Simple Turkey Pot Pie

Cathy Rutz
Andover, KS

Topped with buttermilk biscuits, this pot pie is surprisingly simple to prepare, yet every bit as tasty as you'd expect.

16-oz. pkg. frozen mixed vegetables, thawed and drained
2 14-3/4 oz. cans creamed corn
10-3/4 oz. can cream of mushroom soup
3/4 c. milk
2 c. cooked turkey, chopped
2 12-oz. tubes refrigerated buttermilk biscuits, quartered

Mix vegetables, corn, soup, milk and turkey; pour into a 13"x9" baking pan sprayed with non-stick vegetable spray. Top with biscuits; bake at 350 degrees for 35 to 40 minutes, or until biscuits are golden. Serves 6.

Set the table with a kids-eye view! Arrange stickers on a plastic tablecloth or cut placemats from kraft paper and set out some crayons. Have kids "dress up" for dinner and wear beads, feather boas and hats…make family dinners fun and memorable.

Veggie-Chicken Bake

Theresa Currie
Chatham, NJ

A quick-to-fix dish that's rich & creamy.

4 boneless, skinless chicken breasts, cooked and diced
1 c. mayonnaise
1 c. shredded Cheddar cheese
2 10-3/4 oz. cans cream of chicken soup
16-oz. pkg. frozen broccoli and cauliflower, thawed and drained
12-oz. pkg. egg noodles, cooked

Combine chicken, mayonnaise, cheese, soup and vegetables. Spoon into an ungreased 13"x9" baking pan; bake, uncovered, at 350 degrees until heated through. Serve over noodles. Serves 6 to 8.

A tag sale table takes on a new look with just an application of pretty wallpaper! Use one as a handy serving table in the dining room.

Homestyle Turkey & Stuffing

Jo Ann

No leftover turkey on hand? Use chicken instead!

2 c. cooked turkey, cubed
4 c. assorted vegetables, cooked and sliced into bite-size pieces
10-3/4 oz. can cream of celery soup
10-3/4 oz. can cream of potato soup
1 c. milk
1/4 t. dried thyme
1/8 t. pepper
4 c. prepared sage-flavored stuffing mix

Arrange turkey in a shallow, ungreased 3-quart casserole dish; top with vegetables. Stir together soups, milk, thyme and pepper in a bowl; spread over turkey and vegetables. Top with stuffing. Bake at 400 degrees for 25 minutes, until hot. Makes 4 to 6 servings.

Dress up tube biscuits by brushing the tops of each biscuit lightly with beaten egg and arranging a fresh parsley leaf on each. Lightly brush again with egg and bake as directed.

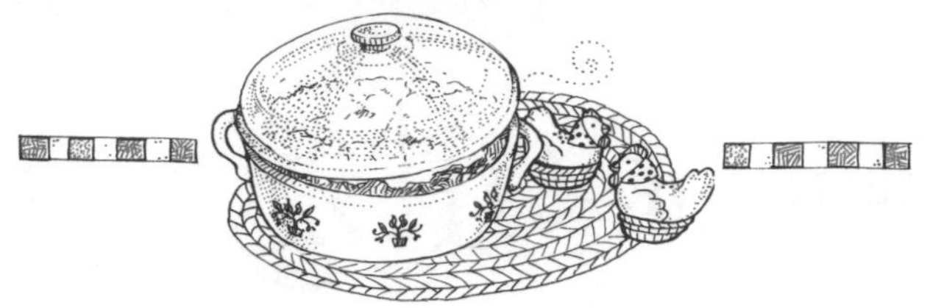

One-Dish Chicken & Gravy

Jennifer Burkum
Maple Grove, MN

My grandma used to make this chicken for us...now whenever I make it, I think of her.

1/4 c. butter, melted
3 lbs. chicken
1/4 c. all-purpose flour
8 pearl onions
4-oz. jar mushroom stems and pieces, drained
2/3 c. evaporated milk
10-3/4 oz. can cream of mushroom soup
1 c. pasteurized processed cheese spread, cubed
3/4 t. salt
1/8 t. pepper
Garnish: paprika

Spread butter in a 12"x8" baking pan; set aside. Coat chicken pieces with flour; arrange in baking dish skin-side down in a single layer. Bake, uncovered, at 425 degrees for 30 minutes. Turn chicken over; bake an additional 15 to 20 minutes until golden. Top with onions and mushrooms; set aside. Combine evaporated milk, soup, cheese, salt and pepper; pour over chicken. Sprinkle with paprika; cover with aluminum foil. Reduce oven to 325 degrees and bake an additional 15 to 20 minutes. Serves 4 to 5.

Wrap a length of wired, sparkly beads around the stems of beverage glasses...a whimsical surprise!

Garlicky Chicken Casserole

Shellye McDaniel
Texarkana, TX

I created this low-carb variation of the chicken enchilada casserole...minus the tortillas!

1/2 c. onion, chopped
2 cloves garlic, pressed
2 T. olive oil
2 12-oz. cans chicken, drained
10-3/4 oz. can cream of mushroom soup
10-oz. can tomatoes with chiles, drained
4 to 6 T. whipping cream
1/2 c. shredded Cheddar cheese
salt and pepper to taste
Garnish: shredded Cheddar cheese, sour cream

In a skillet over medium heat, sauté onion and garlic in oil until onion is translucent. Combine onion mixture and remaining ingredients in a large mixing bowl; stir well. Pour mixture into a lightly greased 13"x9" baking pan. Bake at 350 degrees for 20 to 25 minutes. Garnish as desired with cheese and sour cream. Makes 4 to 6 servings.

Good sound cooking makes a contented home.
-Georges-Auguste Escoffier

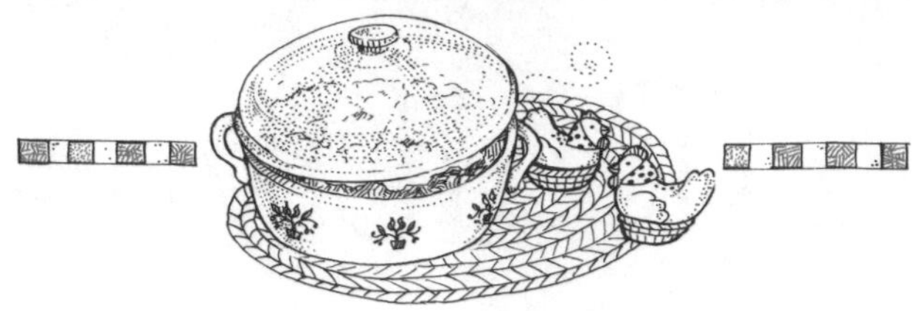

Hot Tamale Casserole

Marlene Darnell
Newport Beach, CA

Once you taste this, you'll make it all the time.

2 lbs. ground turkey
2 1-1/4 oz. pkgs. taco seasoning mix
2 8-1/2 oz. pkgs. corn muffin mix
2 eggs
1 c. milk
2 c. shredded Monterey Jack cheese, divided
1 c. salsa

Brown ground turkey in a skillet over medium heat; drain and add taco seasoning. Set aside. Prepare corn muffin mixes with eggs and milk; mix well. Pour half of the batter into a greased 13"x9" baking pan. Top with ground turkey; layer with one cup cheese. Pour remaining batter over cheese and spread evenly. Bake at 350 degrees for 30 minutes. Remove from oven; spread with salsa and sprinkle with remaining cheese. Return to oven and bake for an additional 10 minutes. Cool for 15 minutes before serving. Serves 4 to 6.

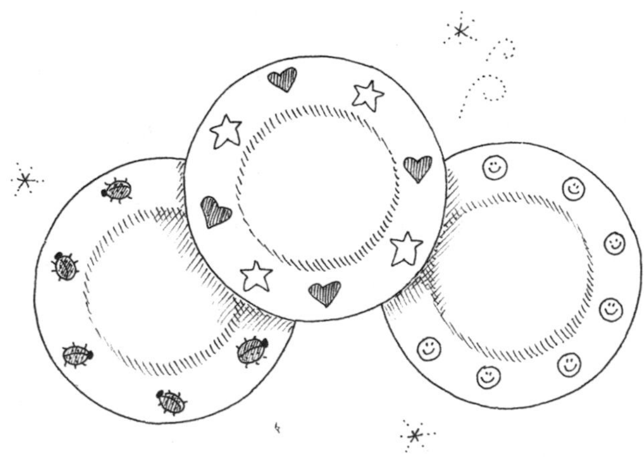

Sometimes paper plates are best when serving little ones, so make 'em fun...surround the plates' edges with stickers!

Poultry

Southwestern Turkey Casserole

Amy Butcher
Columbus, GA

I like to arrange bowls filled with different toppings so everyone can garnish with their favorites...sour cream, chopped cilantro, salsa, chopped green onions and extra shredded cheese.

10-3/4 oz. can cream of chicken soup
10-3/4 oz. can cream of mushroom soup
7-oz. can diced green chiles, drained
1 c. sour cream
16 6-inch corn tortillas, cut into strips
2 c. cooked turkey, diced and divided
8-oz. pkg. shredded Cheddar cheese, divided

Combine soups, chilcs and sour cream in a mixing bowl; set aside. Line the bottom of a 13"x9" baking dish with half the tortilla strips. Top with half the turkey. Spread half the soup mixture over turkey; sprinkle with half the cheese. Repeat layers. Bake at 350 degrees for 30 to 45 minutes. Makes 6 to 8 servings.

Tile squares make great trivets. Found at any home-improvement store, they come in all shapes, sizes and colors.

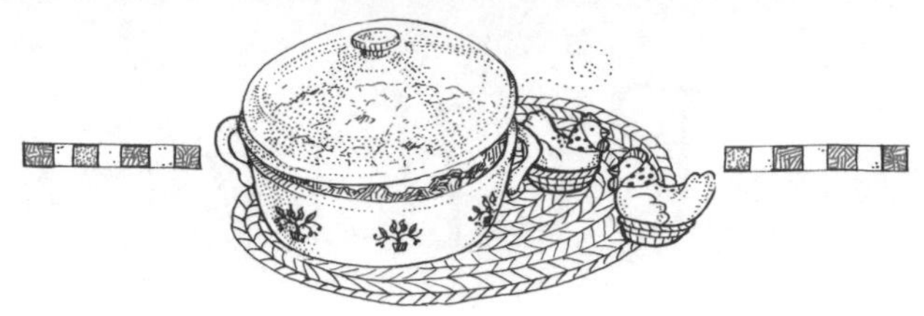

Polynesian Chicken

Norma Burton
Meridian, ID

As my children have grown and started their own families, this favorite recipe is always included in the cookbooks I made for them.

2 lbs. chicken
1/4 c. soy sauce
1 t. ground ginger
1/4 t. pepper
2 T. dried, minced onion
3 T. brown sugar, packed
8-3/4 oz. can pineapple chunks, drained and juice reserved
1/2 c. orange juice
2 t. cornstarch
1/4 c. water
11-oz. can mandarin oranges, drained
4 c. prepared rice

Arrange chicken pieces in a single layer in an ungreased 13"x9" baking pan; set aside. Combine soy sauce, ginger, pepper, onion, brown sugar, reserved pineapple juice and orange juice; pour over chicken. Cover and refrigerate for one hour or overnight, turning once. Bake, covered, at 350 degrees for one hour, or until tender. Remove chicken from baking dish; keep warm on a platter. In a medium saucepan, combine cornstarch and water with pan juices; heat until thickened and bubbly. Stir in pineapple and oranges and warm through; pour over chicken. Serve with cooked rice. Makes 8 servings.

Get out the tiki torches and grass skirts when serving Polynesian Chicken! Play Hawaiian music, make paper flower leis and make it a family dinner to remember.

Poultry

Curried Chicken

Kristina Hughes
Parsonsfield, ME

A tried & true recipe you're sure to enjoy.

1 c. mayonnaise
1 c. all-purpose flour
1 onion, finely chopped
4 to 6 T. curry powder
5 c. chicken broth
2 c. cooked rice, divided
4 to 5 boneless, skinless chicken breasts, cooked, cubed and divided
10-oz. pkg. frozen French-cut green beans, cooked and divided
1 c. soft bread crumbs
1 T. butter

Mix mayonnaise, flour, onion and curry powder in a saucepan. Slowly stir in chicken broth; heat over medium heat until thickened but not boiling. Remove from heat; let cool slightly. In a greased 13"x9" baking pan, layer half the rice, half the chicken, half the green beans and half the sauce; repeat. Gently mix with a fork to let sauce sink in; set aside. Sauté bread crumbs in butter until golden; sprinkle over casserole. Bake at 350 degrees for 20 to 30 minutes, until heated through. Serves 4 to 6.

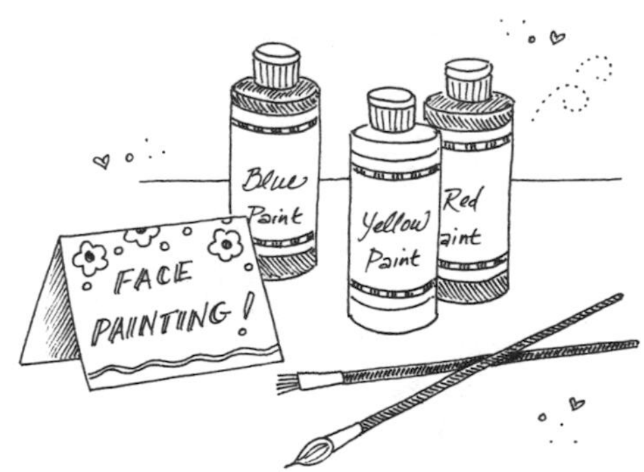

Casseroles are ideal for toting to neighborhood block parties. You'll enjoy catching up with friends while the kids race around playing games. You might even want to set them up a table for face painting...how fun!

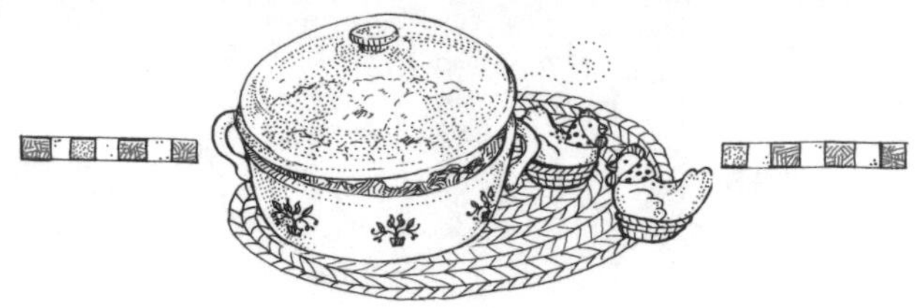

Zippy Chili Casserole

Kelly Alderson
Erie, PA

Just 20 minutes to bake...how speedy!

2 T. butter
2 T. all-purpose flour
2 c. milk
1 T. grated Parmesan cheese
4-1/2 c. prepared wide egg noodles
2 c. turkey, cooked and cubed
1 c. onion, chopped
1-1/2 c. green pepper, chopped
1 T. mustard
1 t. chili powder
2 T. bread crumbs

Melt butter over medium-high heat in a saucepan; sprinkle with flour. Cook, whisking constantly, for 2 minutes. Whisk in milk and cheese. Cook, stirring constantly for 2 minutes until thickened. Remove from heat. Add noodles, turkey, onion, pepper, chili powder and mustard to saucepan; toss to mix well. Spoon mixture into a greased 2-quart casserole dish and sprinkle with bread crumbs. Bake at 375 degrees for 20 minutes, or until golden and bubbly. Serves 6.

Team up! Invite a friend over and prepare several casseroles together. Having someone to chat with makes prep time go quickly and when all the work is done, you'll both have casseroles to freeze...a real timesaver.

Reuben Casserole

Mandy Vandal
Alliance, OH

I've used turkey in place of the expected corned beef...you'll never miss it!

- 20-oz. pkg. frozen shredded hashbrowns, thawed
- 1/4 t. salt
- 1/4 t. pepper
- 1-1/2 lbs. cooked deli turkey, thinly sliced
- 1/4 c. Russian salad dressing
- 16-oz. can sauerkraut, drained
- 8 slices Swiss cheese
- Garnish: extra Russian salad dressing

Sprinkle hashbrowns into a greased 13"x9" baking pan. Sprinkle with salt and pepper; bake at 450 degrees for 15 minutes. Arrange turkey slices over hashbrowns, slightly overlapping; spread with dressing. Spoon sauerkraut over dressing Top with Swiss cheese and bake an additional 15 minutes. Serve with extra dressing. Serves 8.

If there's leftover salad after dinner, use it for a tasty sandwich filling the next day. Split a pita pocket, stuff with salad, chopped chicken or turkey, sliced grapes and drizzle with salad dressing.

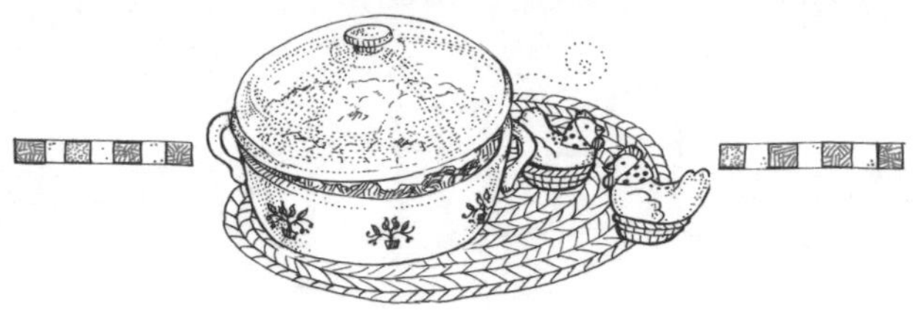

Anytime Enchurritos

Jen Licon-Conner
Gooseberry Patch

This recipe is a natural alongside refried beans and corn cakes.

2 c. turkey, cooked and shredded
1-1/2 c. salsa, divided
1 c. sour cream
2 to 3 T. diced green chiles
8 10-inch flour tortillas
10-3/4 oz. can cream of chicken soup
2 c. shredded Mexican-blend cheese

Combine turkey, 1/2 cup salsa, sour cream and chiles. Spoon turkey mixture into tortillas; roll up and place seam-side down in an ungreased 13"x9" baking pan. Blend together soup and remaining salsa; pour over tortillas. Bake, uncovered, at 350 degrees for 30 minutes. Sprinkle with cheese and bake an additional 5 minutes, or until cheese is melted. Makes 6 to 8 servings.

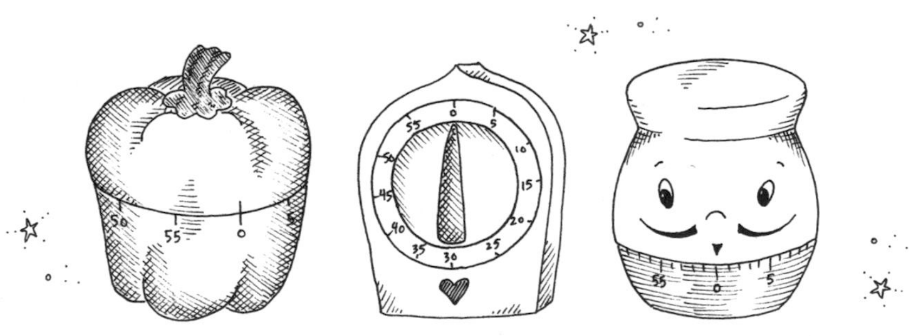

To spice up familiar casserole recipes, use various cheeses like smoked hot pepper or Pepper Jack. Cayenne pepper, chopped pickled jalapeños or fresh jalapeño peppers will also turn up the heat!

Cheesy Chicken & Mac

Myra Barker
Gap, PA

Having company? This overnight dish can be popped in the oven right before guests arrive.

2 c. cooked chicken, diced
2 c. elbow macaroni, uncooked
2 c. milk
2 10-3/4 oz. cans cream of mushroom soup
2 onions, diced
8-oz. pkg. pasteurized processed cheese spread, diced

Mix all ingredients together; spoon into an ungreased 13"x9" baking pan. Refrigerate overnight; bake at 350 degrees for one hour. Serves 6 to 8.

Arrange several tealights on a cake plate for an oh-so-simple centerpiece. Gluing buttons, beads, glitter and ribbon around the metal ring will make them shine.

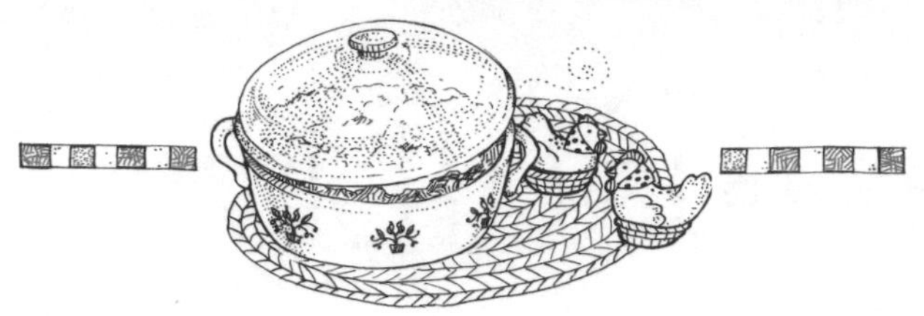

Salsa-Chippy Chicken

Leslie Stimel
Powell, OH

If you like fresh cilantro, try sprinkling a handful on the chicken before pouring the salsa over top. Yum!

2 T. oil
2 T. lime juice
1 t. honey
1 lb. boneless, skinless chicken breast, sliced into 1-inch strips
12 taco shells, crushed
16-oz. jar salsa
2 c. shredded sharp Cheddar cheese

Combine oil, juice and honey in a medium bowl. Dip chicken strips into oil mixture; dredge in crushed taco shells. Arrange in an ungreased 13"x9" baking pan and bake for 25 minutes, until juices run clear. Remove from oven; pour salsa over chicken and sprinkle with cheese. Bake an additional 5 to 7 minutes, or until cheese is melted. Serves 4.

A quick fix…to clean up spilled oil, just cover the spill with a layer of flour. Let sit a few minutes, then wipe up with a paper towel.

Poultry

Sweet & Smoky Chicken

Jennifer Eveland-Kupp
Temple, PA

This is an old Pennsylvania Dutch recipe sure to please dinner guests.

3 lbs. chicken
1 onion, sliced
1/2 c. catsup
1/2 c. molasses
1/4 c. vinegar
1 t. smoke-flavored cooking sauce
1/4 t. pepper

Arrange chicken pieces in a greased 13"x9" baking pan; set aside. Stir together remaining ingredients; pour over chicken. Bake, uncovered, at 350 degrees for one hour, or until chicken juices run clear. Serves 6 to 8.

Light molasses has a sweet, mild taste best for biscuits, waffles and pancakes. But for baking, "dark" molasses, which is less sweet and thicker, is best. In a pinch, they can be interchanged, but to get that robust molasses flavor in a casserole, dark molasses is the best choice.

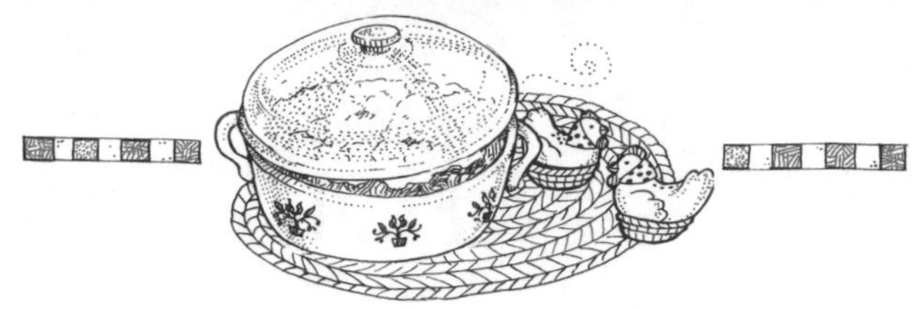

Texas Two-Step Casserole

Sybil Boyter
Duncanville, TX

I created this recipe after experimenting with a variety of peppers, salsas and rubs. I've decided that I really love this combination.

1 lb. ground turkey
1 T. olive oil
1 onion, chopped
3 cloves garlic, minced
1 red chile pepper, finely chopped
1 red pepper, chopped
8-oz. pkg. rotini pasta, cooked
1/4 c. sour cream
1 c. shredded Cheddar cheese, divided
2-1/4 oz. can sliced black olives, drained
1 T. butter, softened
1/2 t. dried parsley
1/2 t. ground cumin
salt and pepper to taste
Optional: 2 T. salsa

In a skillet over medium heat, brown ground turkey in oil; drain. Add onion, garlic and peppers to skillet; sauté until soft. Combine turkey mixture, rotini, sour cream, 1/2 cup cheese, olives, butter, herbs, salt, pepper and salsa, if using, in a greased 13"x9" baking pan. Top with remaining cheese. Bake, covered, at 350 degrees for one hour. Serves 6 to 8.

Check tag sales for vintage dinnerware from hotels, vacation hot spots and diners...they'll really add some flair to dinner!

Seafood

Dijon Salmon Bake

Jaunae Phoenix-Bacon
Macomb, IL

This is so easy and quick, yet everyone thinks that I made a gourmet dinner!

6-oz. pkg. baby spinach, cooked, well-drained and shredded
1-3/4 c. prepared rice
1/2 t. salt, divided
3/4 c. sour cream
1 egg
3 T. grated Parmesan & Romano cheese, divided
1 T. Dijon mustard
1/4 t. pepper
1 lb. boneless, skinless salmon filet, sliced 1/2-inch thick on the diagonal
1/2 t. water

Combine spinach, rice and 1/4 teaspoon salt in a large bowl; set aside. Whisk together sour cream, egg, 2 tablespoons cheese, mustard, remaining salt and pepper in a small bowl. Add all except 4 tablespoons to rice mixture and stir to coat. Place in a greased 1-1/2 quart baking dish; top with salmon. Set aside. Add water to remaining sour cream mixture; mix well and drizzle over salmon. Top with remaining cheese. Bake at 350 degrees for 30 minutes. Let stand 5 minutes before serving. Serves 4.

To keep fish its freshest, put it into a tightly sealed plastic zipping bag, then place inside a bowl filled with ice. Refrigerate and use within a day or two.

Shrimply Divine Casserole

Karen Puchnick
Butler, PA

The combination of spinach and shrimp is perfect pairing!

8-oz. pkg. spinach egg noodles, cooked
3-oz. pkg. cream cheese, cubed
1-1/2 lbs. medium shrimp, peeled and cleaned
1/2 c. butter
10-3/4 oz. can cream of mushroom soup
1 c. sour cream
1/2 c. milk
1/2 c. mayonnaise
1/2 t. mustard
1 T. fresh chives, chopped
Optional: 3/4 c. shredded cheese, any flavor

Place noodles in a lightly greased 13"x9" baking pan. Place cream cheese cubes on hot noodles; set aside. Sauté shrimp in butter, and place all over noodles and cheese. Mix together the remaining ingredients except cheese and pour over shrimp. Sprinkle cheese on top. Bake at 325 degrees for 20 to 30 minutes, or until bubbly and cheese melts. Serves 6.

Fruit kabobs are yummy with seafood dishes! Spear frozen berries, pineapple chunks, melon balls or strawberries on wooden skewers...so simple.

Chopstick Tuna

Anna McMaster
Portland, OR

Chow mein noodles and cashews give this casserole its deliciously different crunch!

10-3/4 oz. can cream of mushroom soup
5 T. water
3-oz. can chow mein noodles, divided
1/4 c. onion, chopped
6-oz. can tuna, drained
1/2 c. salted cashews, chopped
1 c. celery, chopped

In a medium bowl, combine soup and water. Add half the noodles and remaining ingredients. Toss well and place in an ungreased 11"x7" baking pan. Sprinkle remaining noodles on top. Bake at 375 degrees for 15 minutes, or until hot and bubbly. Serves 4 to 6.

For a dinnertime surprise, serve up individual servings of crispy salads in hollowed-out red or green peppers.

Lemony Cod Bake

Laura Strausberger
Roswell, GA

A simple, tried & true recipe you can count on.

4 to 6 cod fillets
1/2 c. butter, melted
2 T. lemon juice
1/4 c. onion, minced
1-1/2 t. Worcestershire sauce
1/4 t. salt
1/4 t. dried parsley

Place fish in an ungreased 13"x9" baking pan. Combine remaining ingredients and pour over fish. Bake at 350 degrees for 30 minutes, until fish flakes. Serves 4 to 6.

A snappy seafood sauce! Just use measurements to suit your taste. Add lemon juice, lemon zest and capers to a mixture of mayonnaise and sour cream. Sprinkle with a dash of salt & pepper.

Creamy Salmon Manicotti

Cheri Maxwell
Gulf Breeze, FL

Salmon topped with Alfredo sauce...superb!

16-oz. container ricotta cheese
7.1-oz. pkg. skinless, boneless pink salmon, flaked
1 egg, beaten
8 prepared manicotti shells
16-oz. jar Alfredo sauce
Garnish: dill weed

In a medium bowl, combine ricotta, salmon and egg until well mixed. Using a small spoon, fill each manicotti shell with the ricotta mixture; if there is any mixture left, stir into sauce. Place filled manicotti in a lightly greased 11"x7" baking pan. Pour sauce over manicotti. Sprinkle with dill. Bake covered at 350 degrees for 35 to 40 minutes.
Serves 4 to 6.

Mess-less manicotti! Place manicotti filling in a pastry bag, then pipe into cooked shells. So much easier than trying to spoon the filling into shells.

Dilly Tuna Casserole

Geneva Rogers
Gillette, WY

You can also substitute shrimp or crab for a whole new flavor.

1/2 c. mayonnaise
1/2 c. milk
10-3/4 oz. can cream of mushroom soup
1 c. shredded Cheddar cheese
1/2 t. dill weed
6-oz. pkg. rotini pasta, cooked
6-oz. can tuna, drained
1 c. potato chips, crushed

Combine mayonnaise and milk; stir in soup, cheese and dill. Gently stir in cooked pasta and tuna. Pour into an ungreased 1-1/2 quart casserole dish. Cover and bake at 350 degrees for 30 minutes. Uncover and sprinkle with potato chips; bake an additional 5 minutes. Serves 6.

Just for fun, try a new flavor of pasta in a favorite casserole recipe...sun-dried tomato-basil, lemon pepper, roasted garlic & parsley or jalapeño. So many flavorful choices!

Crab & Shrimp Delight

Brad Daugherty
Gooseberry Patch

You'll get requests for this recipe!

10-3/4 oz. can cream of shrimp soup
1 c. mayonnaise
1 c. milk
1/2 lb. crabmeat
1/2 lb. cooked tiny shrimp
8-oz. pkg. angel hair pasta, uncooked and broken up
8-oz. pkg. shredded Cheddar cheese

In a large bowl, combine soup, mayonnaise and milk. Stir until smooth; stir in crabmeat, shrimp and pasta. Spoon into an ungreased 13"x9" baking pan. Sprinkle top with cheese. Cover and bake at 350 degrees for 35 minutes, until hot and bubbly. Serves 6 to 8.

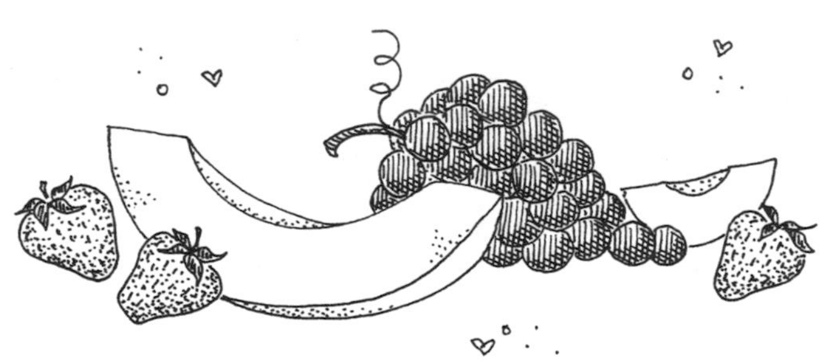

Try serving homemade fruit dip with apple slices, grapes, melon wedges and strawberries. What a refreshing side dish and this dip recipe is a snap! Stir together a 16-ounce container of sour cream, 1/4 cup sugar and 2 teaspoons vanilla extract.

Seafood

Shrimp-Stuffed Pasta Shells

Melody Taynor
Everett, WA

More hot pepper sauce will give this an added dash of heat.

- 1 c. ricotta cheese
- 4-oz. can tiny shrimp, drained
- 1 t. hot pepper sauce
- 1/2 t. lemon-pepper seasoning
- 5-oz. pkg. jumbo pasta shells, cooked
- 1.8-oz. pkg. lemon-dill sauce seasoning mix
- 1 c. water
- 1/2 c. milk
- Garnish: grated Parmesan cheese

In a medium bowl, combine ricotta cheese, shrimp, pepper sauce and lemon-pepper. Evenly divide filling among shells; place in an ungreased 11"x7" baking pan. Set aside. In a medium saucepan, gradually combine sauce mix, water and milk. Cook over medium heat until mixture comes to a boil; stir constantly. Boil for one minute. Pour over shells; sprinkle with cheese. Cover and bake at 350 degrees for 20 minutes, or until hot. Serves 4.

Who says teacups need to be tucked away on a shelf? Insert cup hooks along the top of a window and hang teacups side-by-side. What a sweet "valance" for a cozy kitchen.

Elliott's Tuna Noodle Casserole

Josette Macaluso
El Toro, CA

No recipe box is complete without this fabulous classic.

3 10-3/4 oz. cans cream of mushroom soup
8-oz. pkg. cream cheese, softened
1 c. shredded Muenster cheese
2 6-oz. cans tuna, drained
12-oz. pkg. egg noodles, cooked

Blend soup, cheeses and tuna; fold in noodles. Place in an ungreased 2-1/2 quart casserole dish. Bake at 350 degrees for 45 minutes, or until hot and bubbly. Serves 6 to 8.

Smooth river rocks are perfect plant markers. Use a permanent black marker to write the plant names right on the surface of the rocks.

Seafood

Orange Roughy Au Gratin

Annette Ingram
Grand Rapids, MI

A golden, buttery bread crumb topping makes this casserole one of the best.

- 2 lbs. orange roughy fillets
- 10-3/4 oz. can cream of mushroom soup
- 1/4 c. milk
- 1/2 c. grated Parmesan cheese
- 1-1/2 c. bread crumbs
- 3 T. butter, melted

Arrange fish in a greased 13"x9" baking pan; set aside. Combine soup with milk in a saucepan over medium-low heat; heat through. Pour soup mixture over fish; sprinkle with cheese. Toss together bread crumbs and butter; sprinkle over cheese. Bake at 350 degrees for 10 to 15 minutes, until fish is flaky and cooked though. Serves 6 to 8.

Change the flavor of a seafood casserole just by trying a different type of fish in the recipe. Mild-flavored fish would be cod, flounder or haddock, while stronger flavors would include swordfish, tuna, salmon or mackerel.

Cajun Crab Casserole

Elizabeth Blackstone
Racine, WI

So easy to prepare, this is one of my weeknight favorites.

8-oz. can crabmeat, drained
10-3/4 oz. can cream of mushroom soup
1/2 c. prepared herb-flavored stuffing mix
1/2 c. green pepper, chopped
1/2 c. celery, chopped
1/2 c. mayonnaise
hot pepper sauce and Cajun seasoning to taste

Combine all ingredients. Pour into a greased 1-1/2 quart casserole dish. Bake at 350 degrees for 45 minutes to one hour, until hot and bubbly. Serves 4.

An old enamelware saucepan keeps twine handy for wrapping up bundles of fresh herbs or tying on gift tags. The pan keeps the twine from tangling and rolling out of sight, and the handle keeps it easy to grab & go!

Swiss Seafood Lasagna

Kendall Hale
Lynn, MA

An elegant twist on the traditional lasagna recipe.

2 14-1/2 oz. cans stewed tomatoes, chopped
1/2 c. sliced mushrooms
1/2 t. dried oregano
1/2 t. onion powder
1/8 t. salt
1/8 t. pepper
1/2 c. frozen cooked small shrimp, thawed and cleaned
3 T. margarine
3 T. all-purpose flour
1-3/4 c. milk
1 c. shredded Swiss cheese
8-oz. pkg. crabmeat, chopped
1/4 c. white wine or chicken broth
8 strips prepared lasagna
1/4 c. grated Parmesan cheese

Combine undrained tomatoes, mushrooms, oregano, onion powder, salt and pepper in a medium saucepan; bring to boiling. Reduce heat and simmer, uncovered, about 20 minutes or until thickened. Stir in shrimp; set aside. Melt margarine in a second medium saucepan; stir in flour. Add milk; cook and stir over medium heat until thickened and bubbly. Cook and stir an additional minute. Stir in Swiss cheese until melted; stir in crabmeat and wine or broth. Layer half of the shrimp sauce, half of the lasagna strips and half of the cheese sauce in an ungreased 2-quart rectangular casserole dish. Repeat layers. Top with Parmesan cheese. Bake, uncovered, at 350 degrees for about 25 minutes or until heated through. Let stand 15 minutes before serving. Makes 6 to 8 servings.

Asparagus makes such an elegant side dish and is surprisingly simple to prepare! Simply place the spears on a sheet of aluminum foil, drizzle with olive oil and sprinkle with garlic salt. Grill or broil about 5 minutes or until tender.

Navy Crab Bake

Wendy Lee Paffenroth
Pine Island, NY

They'll be coming back for more...better make an extra!

2 to 3 slices bread, crusts removed, cubed
1 to 2 T. milk
1 to 1-1/2 lbs. crabmeat, flaked
1 t. seafood seasoning
1/8 t. salt
1 T. mayonnaise
1/4 t. Worcestershire sauce
1 T. fresh parsley, chopped
1 egg, beaten
1 T. baking powder
Optional: shredded mozzarella cheese

In a medium bowl, combine bread and enough milk to moisten. Add remaining ingredients except cheese; mix well. Pour into a lightly greased 11"x7" baking pan. Bake at 325 degrees for 30 minutes, or until heated through. Sprinkle with cheese, if using; return to oven until cheese is melted. Serves 4 to 6.

A little red wagon makes a great carry-all for any outdoor gathering. Fill it with pails of perky blooms or fill it with crushed ice and bottles of soda, water or juice boxes.

Oh-So-Easy Fish Bake

Athena Colegrove
Big Springs, TX

For this versatile recipe, you can try red snapper or orange roughy if you'd like.

10-oz. pkg. frozen chopped spinach, thawed and well drained
1 c. shredded Cheddar cheese, divided
1/3 c. dry bread crumbs, divided
1 egg, beaten
1 lb. cod fillets
salt and pepper to taste

In a medium bowl, mix spinach, 1/2 cup cheese, 5 tablespoons bread crumbs and egg. Spread the mixture into a lightly greased 11"x7" baking pan. Arrange cod fillets on top of spinach mixture; add salt and pepper. Top with remaining bread crumbs and cheese. Cover and bake at 325 degrees for 20 minutes, or until fish flakes easily with a fork. Serves 4.

Cleaning a casserole baking dish can be a breeze! Fill the sink with hot, soapy water, then put the empty casserole dish in to soak while enjoying dessert.

Herbed Seafood Casserole

Rita Morgan
Pueblo, CO

This rich seafood dish is tasty with garlic bread and spinach salad.

1 lb. frozen cooked medium shrimp, thawed, cleaned and chopped
1/2 lb. lobster, chopped
1/4 lb. crabmeat, chopped
4-oz. can sliced mushrooms, drained
1/4 c. butter
1/4 c. all-purpose flour
2 c. milk
salt and pepper to taste
1/4 t. paprika
2 t. fresh chives, snipped
2 t. fresh parsley, finely chopped
2 T. white wine or chicken broth
4 T. grated Parmesan cheese

Combine shrimp, lobster, crabmeat and mushrooms in a greased 1-1/2 quart casserole dish; set aside. In a medium saucepan, melt butter over medium-low heat; stir in flour until smooth and bubbly. Gradually add milk, stirring constantly. Continue to cook over low heat, stirring constantly, until thickened and bubbly. Stir in seasonings and wine or broth. Gently stir sauce into seafood mixture; sprinkle with Parmesan cheese. Bake at 350 degrees for 20 minutes; place under a broiler for one minute until golden on top. Serves 4.

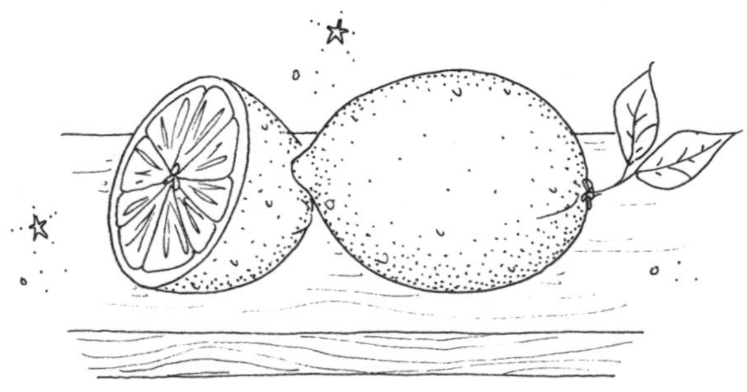

Keep cutting boards smelling fresh by simply rubbing them thoroughly with lemon wedges. Works for hands too!

Seafood

Deep Sea Delight

Carrie O'Shea
Marina Del Ray, CA

This scrumptious recipe is filled with 4 types of seafood!

3 T. plus 1-1/2 t. butter, divided
1 c. onion, chopped
1-1/2 c. celery, chopped
2-1/2 c. milk
6 T. all-purpose flour
1/4 lb. Cheddar cheese, sliced
1/2 t. salt
1/2 t. pepper
1/4 lb. crabmeat, flaked
1/4 lb. lobster, flaked
1/4 lb. medium shrimp, peeled and cleaned
1/4 lb. scallops

Melt 3 tablespoons butter in a skillet; sauté onion and celery until tender. Set aside. Heat milk in a saucepan over medium heat. Mix in flour and remaining butter until well blended. Gradually blend cheese into mixture; add salt and pepper. In a medium bowl, combine onion mixture with cheese sauce mixture. Toss in seafood; transfer to a greased 11"x7" baking pan. Bake at 350 degrees for 25 minutes, until seafood is opaque and surface is lightly golden. Serves 4.

Only using part of an onion? The remaining half will stay fresh for weeks when rubbed with butter or oil and stored in the refrigerator.

Zesty Creole Bake

Zoe Bennett
Columbia, SC

This recipe is good when you're in the mood for something a little tangy!

3 c. water
1-1/2 c. instant rice, uncooked
1/4 c. butter
1 onion, chopped
1 clove garlic, minced
2 stalks celery, chopped
1 green pepper, chopped
1/4 c. all-purpose flour
2 c. milk
1 t. salt
1/4 t. pepper
1/2 t. hot pepper sauce
1/2 c. chili sauce
1 lb. cod fillets
2 tomatoes, sliced

Bring water to a boil in a saucepan; add rice and stir. Reduce heat; cover and simmer for 20 minutes. Set aside. Melt butter in a skillet over medium heat. Add onion and garlic; cook until tender, about 4 minutes. Add celery and pepper; cook for 3 minutes until tender but not browned. Add flour and stir well; cook for an additional 3 minutes. Stir in milk and bring just to a boil. Stir in salt, pepper, hot sauce and chili sauce. Place rice in a greased 13"x9" baking pan. Arrange fish fillets over rice in a single layer. Place sliced tomatoes over fish; pour sauce over the top. Bake at 400 degrees for 20 minutes, or until fish flakes easily with fork. Serves 4.

If you're making rice for dinner, why not make some extra? Frozen in one-cup serving containers, it's handy to reheat later in the week for a quick lunch or dinner.

Montana Baked Halibut

Lisa Wahl
Scobey, MT

I like to garnish servings with freshly chopped parsley or chives.

3 lbs. halibut fillets
3 T. butter, softened and divided
salt and pepper to taste
4 slices bacon
1/2 c. grated Parmesan cheese
1 c. sour cream
2 t. lemon juice
1/3 c. cornbread croutons, crushed

Rub halibut with 2 tablespoons butter; add salt and pepper. Arrange bacon in an ungreased 13"x9" baking pan; place halibut on bacon. Mix cheese, sour cream and lemon juice together; spread over halibut. Set aside. Melt remaining butter in a saucepan over low heat; remove from heat and add croutons. Toss to coat; sprinkle over halibut. Bake at 350 degrees for 25 to 30 minutes, depending on thickness of halibut. Serves 6 to 8.

To freshen cooking pans after preparing fish in them, simply fill the pan with equal parts vinegar and water. Bring to a boil for 5 minutes, let cool, then wash the pan with hot, soapy water.

Seafood Bisque Casserole

Linda Stone
Cookeville, TN

Oodles of seafood in a velvety cream sauce.

7 T. butter, divided
1/2 lb. small shrimp, peeled and cleaned
1/2 lb. crabmeat
1/2 lb. scallops
1 T. shallots, chopped
10 T. sherry or chicken broth, divided
1/2 t. salt
1/4 t. pepper
3 T. all-purpose flour
1-1/2 c. milk
Garnish: bread crumbs, grated Parmesan cheese

Melt 4 tablespoons butter in a large skillet over medium heat. Add seafood and shallots; sauté for 5 minutes. Sprinkle with 6 tablespoons sherry or broth, salt and pepper; set aside. In a small saucepan, melt remaining butter; add flour, stirring to thicken. Add milk and remaining sherry; stir until smooth. Combine sauce and seafood mixture and place in a lightly greased 13"x9" baking pan. Sprinkle with bread crumbs and Parmesan; bake at 400 degrees for 30 minutes. Serves 6 to 8.

Serve seafood as a scrumptious appetizer before dinner. Whip up Mint Pesto Sauce for dipping. Combine 1 clove garlic, 2 tablespoons toasted almonds, 2 cups fresh mint leaves, 1/4 cup olive oil, 1/3 cup plain yogurt and 1 tablespoon lemon juice in a food processor. Process until well blended.

Creamy Seafood Enchiladas

Kristie Rigo
Friedens, PA

My family flips when I make these creamy enchiladas!

12-oz. pkg. imitation crabmeat, flaked
10 10-inch flour tortillas
3 T. butter
1 onion, minced
2 cloves garlic, minced
1 t. coriander
1/2 t. salt
1/2 t. pepper
8-oz. container sour cream
3 T. all-purpose flour
14-1/2 oz. can chicken broth
2 4-oz. cans diced green chiles
1-1/2 c. shredded Monterey Jack cheese, divided

Place crabmeat in a medium bowl; set aside. Wrap tortillas in aluminum foil; bake at 350 degrees for 10 minutes, until softened. Set aside. Heat butter in a medium saucepan; add onion, garlic, coriander, salt and pepper and heat until onion is transparent. Set aside. Combine sour cream and flour in a medium bowl; stir in broth. Add sour cream mixture and chiles to onion mixture in saucepan; cook over medium heat until thick and bubbly. Remove from heat; add 1/2 cup cheese. Add one cup of hot mixture to crabmeat; divide among softened tortillas, placing filling in middle of each tortilla. Roll up tortillas; arrange seam-side down in a greased 13"x9" baking pan and top with remaining sour cream mixture. Bake, covered, at 350 degrees for 30 to 35 minutes, until heated through. Sprinkle with remaining cheese. Bake, uncovered, for 5 additional minutes, until cheese is melted. Let stand 5 minutes before serving. Makes 4 to 6 servings.

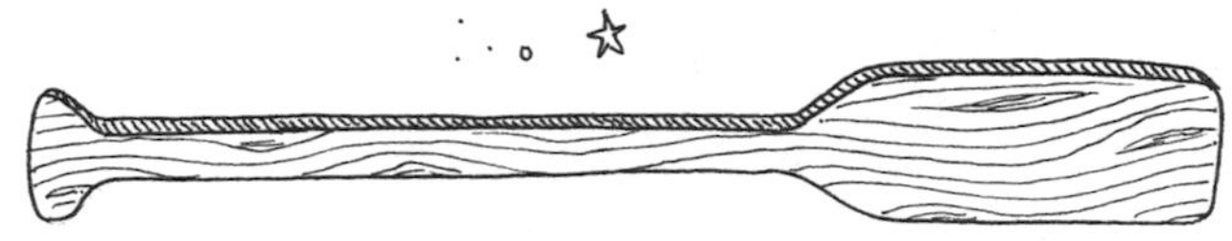

Where even the teakettle sings from happiness, that is home.
-Ernestine Schumann-Heink

Shrimp Monterey

Donna Nowicki
Center City, MN

Garlic and shrimp...what a combination!

2 cloves garlic, minced
2 T. butter
2 lbs. medium shrimp, peeled and cleaned
1/2 c. white wine or chicken broth
2 c. shredded Monterey Jack cheese
2 T. fresh parsley, minced

In a skillet over medium heat, sauté garlic in butter for one minute. Add shrimp; cook for 4 to 5 minutes, or until pink. Using a slotted spoon, transfer shrimp to a greased 11"x7" baking pan; set aside and keep warm. Pour wine or chicken broth into the skillet; bring to a boil. Cook and stir for 5 minutes. Pour over shrimp; top with cheese and parsley. Bake, uncovered, at 350 degrees for 10 minutes, or until cheese is melted. Serves 4 to 6.

Make buttery crescent rolls even better by sprinkling a little cheese on them before rolling up.

Almond-Topped Salmon

Tina Wright
Atlanta, GA

Here's an elegant dinner for any occasion.

1/2 c. onion, finely chopped
2 T. butter
10-3/4 oz. can cream of mushroom soup
8-oz. container sour cream
1/2 t. garlic salt
8-oz. pkg. spaghetti, uncooked
12-oz. can salmon, drained and flaked
10-oz. frozen chopped broccoli, cooked
2 T. sherry or chicken broth
1/4 c. grated Parmesan cheese
1/4 c. sliced almonds

In a medium saucepan over medium heat, cook onion in butter for 5 minutes, until tender. Add soup, sour cream and garlic salt; heat and stir. Set aside. Cook half the spaghetti according to package directions, reserving the rest of another recipe. Fold into soup mixture with salmon, broccoli and sherry or broth. Place in a greased 1-1/2 quart casserole dish. Sprinkle with cheese and top with almonds. Bake at 350 degrees for 20 to 25 minutes. Serves 4 to 6.

Slice a garlic clove in half and rub the insides of individual salad bowls...adds just a touch of garlic flavor.

Shrimp & Feta Casserole

Jill Valentine
Jackson, TN

Chunky salsa is the secret ingredient in this savory dinner.

2 eggs
1 c. evaporated milk
1 c. plain yogurt
3 oz. pkg. crumbled feta cheese
2 c. shredded Swiss cheese
1/4 c. fresh parsley, chopped
1 t. dried basil
1 t. dried oregano
4 cloves garlic, minced
8-oz. pkg. angel hair pasta, cooked
16-oz. jar chunky salsa
1 lb. medium shrimp, peeled, cleaned and divided
8-oz. pkg. shredded mozzarella cheese

In a medium bowl, combine the first 9 ingredients; set aside. Spread half the pasta in a greased 13"x9" baking pan. Cover with salsa; add half the shrimp. Spread remaining pasta over shrimp; top with egg mixture. Add remaining shrimp and top with mozzarella cheese. Bake at 350 degrees for 30 minutes. Remove from oven and let stand for 5 minutes before serving. Serves 6 to 8.

Blenders are a great help in the kitchen. Use them to crush ice, pureé vegetables or whip together ingredients for sauces. To clean one quickly, just add warm water and a little dish soap. Blend for a few seconds; rinse and dry.

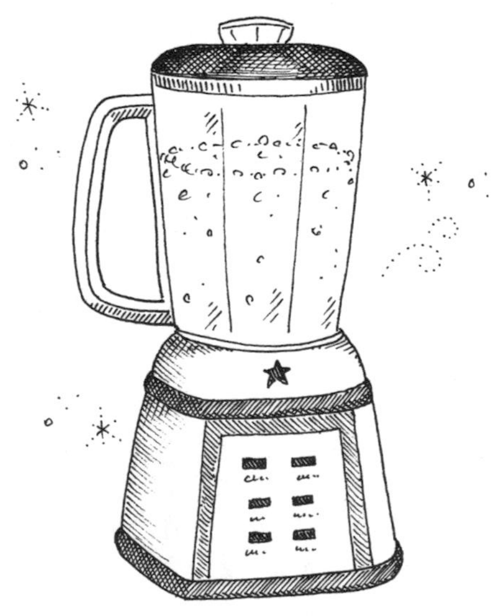

Parmesan Fish Bake

Kerry Mayer
Dunham Springs, LA

For a switch, use wheat germ instead of bread crumbs.

1/4 c. milk
2 t. salt
1/2 c. dry bread crumbs
1/2 t. paprika
1/4 c. grated Parmesan cheese
2 lbs. haddock fillets
2 to 3 T. butter, melted

Blend together milk and salt in a shallow bowl. Combine bread crumbs, paprika and cheese in another bowl. Dip fillets into milk mixture; dredge in crumb mixture. Arrange in a greased 11"x7" baking pan. Drizzle butter over fillets. Bake at 375 degrees for 25 to 30 minutes, depending on thickness of fillets. Serves 6.

Out of bread crumbs for a casserole? Just substitute crushed herb-flavored stuffing mix instead and it will be just as tasty.

Ostiones en Cazuela

Regina Wickline
Pebble Beach, CA

The name means Oyster Casserole...the taste is out of this world!

1 pt. oysters, drained
2 tomatoes, chopped
1/2 c. half-and-half, divided
2 c. cracker crumbs
1/2 c. butter, melted
1/2 t. salt
1/2 t. ground cumin
1/4 t. allspice
1/8 t. cayenne pepper
Garnish: lemon or lime wedges

Combine oysters and tomatoes; arrange in an ungreased 11"x7" baking pan. Pour 1/4 cup half-and-half over top. Combine crumbs, butter and seasonings; sprinkle over oyster mixture. Pour remaining half-and-half over crumb mixture. Bake, uncovered, at 375 degrees for 30 minutes. Garnish with lemon or lime wedges. Serves 4.

Serve lemon and lime wedges with seafood casseroles...their citrus taste is perfect pairing with seafood. Guests can squeeze on as much or as little as they'd like.

Seafood

Southern-Style Shrimp & Rice

Claire Bertram
Lexington, KY

An updated version of an old-fashioned favorite.

3/4 c. butter, divided
1 onion, sliced
8-oz. pkg. sliced mushrooms
1/4 c. green pepper, diced
2 c. prepared long-grain and wild rice
1-1/2 lbs. medium shrimp, peeled and cleaned
1 T. Worcestershire sauce
hot pepper sauce to taste
salt and pepper to taste
1/2 c. all-purpose flour
1-1/2 c. chicken broth
1/2 c. white wine or chicken broth

In a large heavy skillet, melt 1/4 cup butter over medium heat. Add onion, mushrooms, and pepper; sauté for 8 minutes. Add rice; toss until well blended and spread across bottom of a greased 2-quart casserole dish. Set aside. In a medium mixing bowl, combine shrimp, sauces, salt and pepper. Arrange evenly over vegetable mixture; set aside. Melt remaining butter over medium heat in a saucepan; add flour and whisk for one minute. Add broth and wine or additional broth. Whisk until well blended and slightly thickened; pour evenly over shrimp. Bake at 350 degrees for 25 minutes, until bubbly. Serves 6.

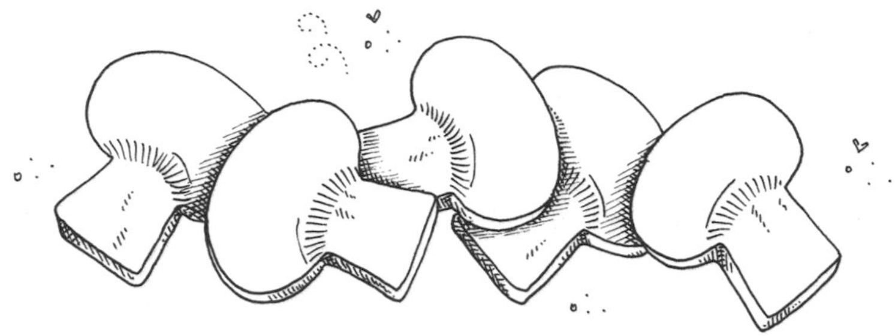

Broth is an easy substitution for wine in recipes. Use beef broth for red wine and chicken broth for white.

Coquilles St. Jacques

Maria Kinsella
St. Louis, MO

Birthdays in our family have always been an occasion for a gathering. Each person, since their childhood days, has had the delight of choosing his or her special dinner for their big day. Without exception, this recipe for French Sea Scallops has always been a favorite.

1 lb. scallops, sliced into bite-size pieces
2 c. water
juice of 1 lemon
1 bay leaf
1/2 t. hot pepper sauce
1 t. dried, minced onion
3 T. butter
2 T. all-purpose flour
1 t. salt
1 c. light cream
2 egg yolks
1/2 c. grated Swiss cheese
2 T. white wine or chicken broth
Garnish: paprika
2 to 3 c. prepared rice

Place scallops in a saucepan; add water, lemon juice, bay leaf, hot pepper sauce and onion. Simmer for 5 minutes; drain and set aside. In another pan, melt butter over low heat and stir in hot pepper sauce, flour and salt. Gradually stir in cream. Cook over low heat, stirring constantly, until mixture thickens and comes to a boil. Add a small amount of egg yolk, stirring constantly, and then remaining egg yolks. Add cheese, wine or broth and scallops. Place in a lightly greased 11"x7" baking pan; sprinkle with paprika. Bake at 350 degrees for 10 to 15 minutes until golden. Serve with rice. Serves 4.

I don't like gourmet cooking or "this" cooking or "that" cooking. I like "good" cooking.
-James Beard

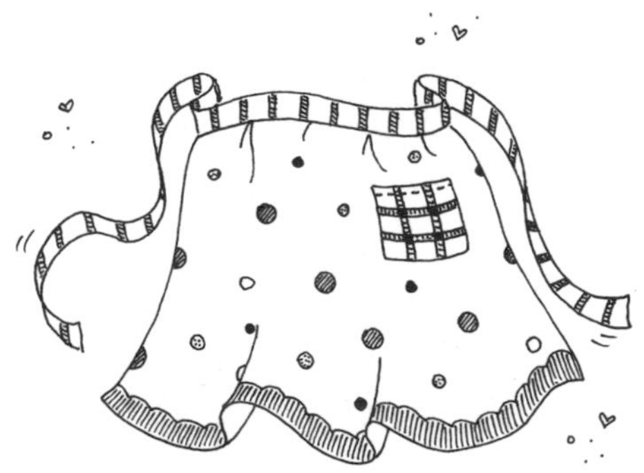

Rotini-Tuna Casserole

Tammy Rowe
Bellevue, OH

You can use almost any canned "cream of" soup in this versatile casserole recipe.

10-3/4 oz. can cream of chicken soup
1-1/4 c. milk
16-oz. pkg. rainbow rotini pasta, cooked
14-1/2 oz. can mixed vegetables, drained
6-oz. can tuna, drained
8-oz. can sliced mushrooms, drained
2-oz. jar pimentos, drained
salt and pepper to taste
1 t. dried parsley
1/2 c. shredded Cheddar cheese
1/2 c. potato chips, crushed

In a large bowl, mix soup and milk together. Add pasta, vegetables, tuna, mushrooms, pimentos and seasonings; mix well. Pour into an ungreased 2-quart casserole dish; top with cheese and potato chip crumbs. Bake at 350 degrees for 30 minutes, or until heated through. Serves 6 to 8.

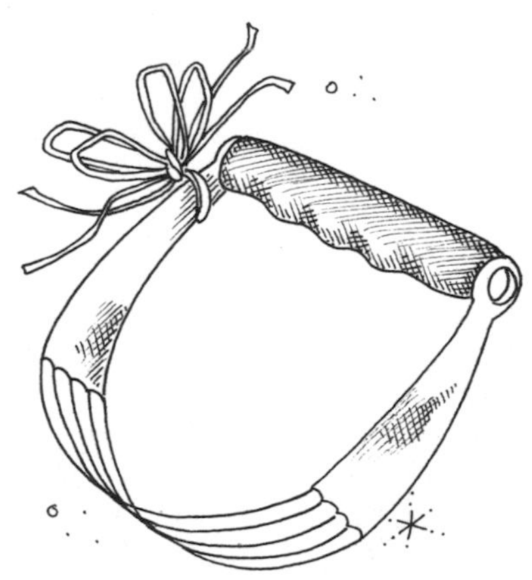

To easily crumble tuna for casserole dishes, just use a pastry blender!

Mock Oyster Casserole

Dale Duncan
Waterloo, LA

One of our tastiest recipes...no one will miss the oysters!

1 eggplant, peeled and sliced into 1-inch cubes
1/2 c. butter, melted
1-1/2 c. buttery round cracker crumbs
1 egg, beaten
6-1/2 oz. can minced clams, drained and liquid reserved
salt, pepper and hot pepper sauce to taste

Drop eggplant into boiling water for 3 minutes. Drain well; set aside. Add butter to cracker crumbs; mix well. Reserve 1/3 cup crumb mixture for topping. Gently mix beaten egg, clams and eggplant. Add crumb mixture, salt, pepper and hot pepper sauce. Add just enough reserved clam liquid to make moist, but not soupy. Pour into a greased 11"x7" baking pan. Top with reserved crumbs and bake at 350 degrees for 45 minutes. Serves 4 to 6.

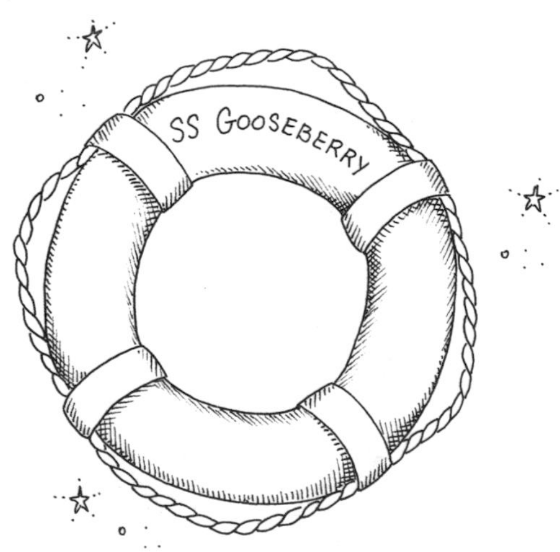

Bring a little of the beach inside. Slip some tiny seashells on lengths of copper wire, then wrap around the stems of glasses...so pretty!

Crab-Stuffed Eggplant

Karen Pilcher
Burleson, TX

Serving this for dinner is a treat for the whole family...we love it.

1-1/2 lb. eggplant
5-1/2 T. butter, divided
1/2 c. bread crumbs
1/4 c. grated Parmesan cheese
6 to 8 green onions, chopped
2 T. fresh parsley, chopped
1 lb. jumbo lump crabmeat
1/4 t. salt
1/4 t. pepper
1/2 c. mayonnaise
1 T. all-purpose flour
1/2 c. whipping cream
1 T. Worcestershire sauce

Cover eggplant with water; boil for 15 minutes. Drain. When cool enough to handle, cut in half lengthwise and remove pulp, leaving a shell 1/4-inch thick. Chop pulp and reserve. Arrange shells in a lightly greased 13"x9" baking pan; set aside. Melt one tablespoon butter in a large skillet; add bread crumbs and sauté until golden. Add cheese and stir to coat; set aside. In a separate skillet, melt 4 tablespoons butter. Add green onions and parsley; sauté for 2 minutes. Add eggplant pulp and remaining ingredients, except remaining butter. Sauté eggplant mixture, stirring constantly, for 3 minutes. Spoon filling into each of the shells. Sprinkle with bread crumb mixture; dot with remaining butter. Bake at 400 degrees for 20 minutes. Serves 2 to 4.

An herb bundle makes such a fragrant centerpiece! Bunch together sprigs of dill, rosemary, mint, basil, lavender or thyme in an old-fashioned canning jar. So simple.

Cheesy Shrimp Casserole

Jen Burnham
Delaware, OH

This is an easy recipe...everything is mixed in one bowl and then spooned into the baking dish.

8-oz. pkg. egg noodles, uncooked
3/4 c. milk
1/2 c. mayonnaise
1 T. green onion, chopped
2 4-1/4 oz. cans tiny shrimp, drained
1/3 c. shredded Cheddar cheese
10-3/4 oz. can cream of shrimp soup
1/4 c. celery, diced
1 t. salt
1/4 c. chow mein noodles

Prepare half the egg noodles according to package directions, reserving the rest of another recipe. Combine with remaining ingredients except chow mein noodles in an ungreased 11"x7" baking pan. Bake at 350 degrees for 25 minutes. Top with chow mein noodles and bake for an additional 10 minutes. Serves 4 to 6.

Drizzle Lemon-Dill Butter over warm slices of bread...great served with seafood dishes! Slowly melt 2 cups butter in a small saucepan over low heat. Skim off and discard white foam. Pour butter into a medium size bowl, then stir in 2 tablespoons chopped fresh dill and the zest of 2 lemons.

Garlic Shrimp

Kathy Grashoff
Fort Wayne, IN

Mince fresh garlic for the best flavor. Fresh ingredients really do make a difference in the taste.

24 large shrimp, peeled and cleaned
1/4 c. olive oil
1/4 c. fresh parsley, chopped
3 cloves garlic, minced
1/2 t. red pepper flakes
1/4 t. pepper
1/4 c. butter, melted
1/2 c. dry French bread crumbs
1/2 c. grated Parmesan cheese

Arrange shrimp in an ungreased 11"x7" baking pan; drizzle oil over shrimp. Combine the next 4 ingredients; sprinkle over shrimp. Cover and bake at 300 degrees for 15 minutes. Turn shrimp over. Drizzle with butter; sprinkle with bread crumbs and cheese. Bake, uncovered, for an additional 5 to 10 minutes. Serves 2.

If the kids can't wait until dinner, mix up a quick snack mix for them to munch on. Stir together raisins, candy corn, nuts, chocolate-covered candies and cereal squares in a bowl...enjoy!

Cajun Seafood Fettucine

Sheila Collier
Kingwood, TX

Sometimes this only serves 4!

1-1/2 c. butter, divided
2 8-oz. pkgs. frozen seasoned vegetable blend
garlic powder and Cajun seasoning to taste
1/4 c. all-purpose flour
1 pt. half-and-half
16-oz. pkg. pasteurized processed cheese spread, cubed
1-1/2 lbs. medium shrimp, peeled and cleaned
1-1/2 lbs. crabmeat
12-oz. pkg. egg noodles, cooked
12-oz. pkg. shredded Colby-Jack cheese

Melt 1-1/4 cups butter in a large saucepan; add vegetables and sauté until tender. Sprinkle with garlic powder and Cajun seasoning; set aside. Add enough water to flour to make a thick paste that is still able to be poured; add to skillet. Stir in half-and-half and cheese spread; continue stirring until cheese is melted. Set aside. In a separate skillet, sauté shrimp in remaining butter until no longer pink. Add shrimp and crabmeat to vegetable mixture and let simmer on medium-low heat for 20 minutes. Stir in egg noodles; pour into an ungreased 13"x9" baking pan. Sprinkle with Colby-Jack cheese. Bake at 350 degrees for 20 minutes. Serves 8.

Try this trick for opening stubborn jar lids...just wrap a rubber band around the lid! The rubber band provides just enough friction so your hands grip the lid tightly enough to twist off the lid!

Beef

Family Favorite Beef & Noodles

Michele Nylander
Redding, CA

I used to ask my family what I should make for dinner and got the response, "I dunno!" So one night I invented this dish. Now when I ask, everyone says "I want 'I Dunno' for dinner!"

2 lbs. ground beef
1 T. margarine
15-oz. can tomato sauce
2 cloves garlic, minced
1 t. sugar
1 t. salt
1 t. pepper
8-oz. pkg. cream cheese, softened
8-oz. container sour cream
3/4 c. green onion, sliced
3 c. fettuccine pasta, uncooked
1 c. shredded Cheddar cheese
Garnish: paprika

Brown ground beef in margarine in a skillet; drain. Add tomato sauce, garlic, sugar, salt and pepper; reduce heat and simmer for 20 minutes. In a medium bowl, beat cream cheese with a fork until fluffy; stir in sour cream and onion. Set aside. Cook fettuccine according to package instructions. Layer ingredients as follows in a greased 13"x9" baking pan: beef mixture, cooked fettuccine, cream cheese mixture, Cheddar cheese. Sprinkle with paprika; bake at 350 degrees for 25 to 30 minutes, or until bubbly. Serves 6 to 8.

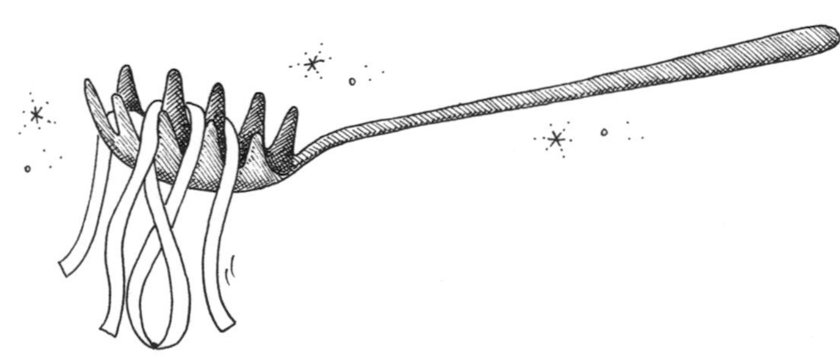

Toss prepared pasta with a little olive oil then set aside to keep warm. When it's time to add the pasta to a favorite casserole recipe, you'll find the oil has kept the pasta from sticking together.

Cheeseburger & Fries Casserole

Shari Miller
Hobart, IN

The recipe name says it all...kids will love it!

2 lbs. ground beef, browned and drained
10-3/4 oz. can golden mushroom soup
10-3/4 oz. can Cheddar cheese soup
20-oz. pkg. frozen crinkle-cut French fries

Combine ground beef and soups; spread in a greased 13"x9" baking pan. Arrange French fries on top. Bake, uncovered, at 350 degrees for 50 to 55 minutes, or until fries are golden. Makes 6 to 8 servings.

If you're adding more than one baking pan to the oven, remember to stagger them on the racks. Placing one pan directly over another won't allow the food to cook evenly in either.

Betty-getti

Mary Nelson
Newberg, OR

This is my Aunt Betty's recipe and she made it for all our family get-togethers. When we were young, my brother, sister and I always called it "Betty-getti!" Now I make it, and my two children love it as much now as I did then.

16-oz. pkg. spaghetti, cooked
1 to 1-1/2 lbs. ground beef, browned and drained
2 10-3/4 oz. cans tomato soup
1/4 c. onion, chopped
1/4 c. green pepper, chopped
1/4 c. celery, chopped
8-oz. pkg. sliced mushrooms
1 clove garlic, minced
Garnish: shredded sharp Cheddar cheese

Mix together all ingredients except cheese; spread in an ungreased 3-quart casserole dish. Sprinkle cheese on top. Bake at 350 degrees for 35 to 45 minutes, until cheese is melted and golden. Serves 6.

No man is lonely while
eating spaghetti:
it requires so
much attention.
-Christopher Morley

Spaghetti Pie

Tina Stidam
Delaware, OH

A recipe kids big and little will love!

12-oz. pkg. spaghetti, uncooked
2 T. butter, softened
1/2 c. grated Parmesan cheese
2 eggs, beaten
1 c. cottage cheese
1 lb. ground beef
1/2 onion, chopped
1/4 c. green pepper, chopped
18-oz. can chopped tomatoes
16-oz. can tomato paste
1 t. sugar
1/2 t. garlic salt
1 t. dried oregano
1/2 c. shredded mozzarella cheese

Prepare half the spaghetti according to package directions, reserving the rest for another recipe. Stir in butter; add Parmesan cheese and eggs. Spoon into a greased 10-inch pie plate; spread cottage cheese over the top. Set aside. In a skillet, brown beef, onion and pepper; drain. Add remaining ingredients except mozzarella cheese. Stir well; pour over cottage cheese layer. Bake at 350 degrees for 20 minutes; sprinkle with mozzarella cheese. Bake for an additional 5 minutes or until cheese melts. Cut into wedges to serve. Makes 6 to 8 servings.

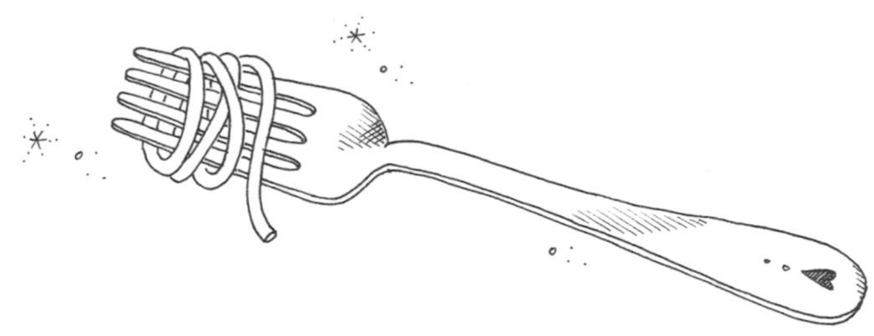

Top slices of warm bread with flavorful Basil-Tomato Butter…it's easy to make. Blend 1/2 cup softened butter with 1/3 cup shredded fresh basil, 1 tablespoon tomato paste and 1/4 teaspoon salt.

Shepherd's Pie

Tami Davidson
Santa Clarita, CA

A classic recipe everyone should have.

4 to 5 potatoes, peeled and boiled
2 T. butter, softened
1/4 to 1/2 c. milk
salt and pepper to taste
1 lb. ground beef
1 tomato, chopped
6 mushrooms, sliced
2 T. fresh parsley, chopped
1 T. tomato paste
1/4 t. Worcestershire sauce
1 c. brown gravy
10-oz. pkg. frozen peas, thawed

Mash potatoes, butter, milk, salt and pepper together; set aside. Brown beef in a skillet; drain. Add tomato, mushrooms, parsley, tomato paste, Worcestershire sauce and gravy; stir to mix. Add peas and simmer for 5 minutes; pour into an ungreased 13"x9" baking pan. Spread mashed potatoes over top; bake at 400 degrees for 40 minutes. Serves 4 to 6.

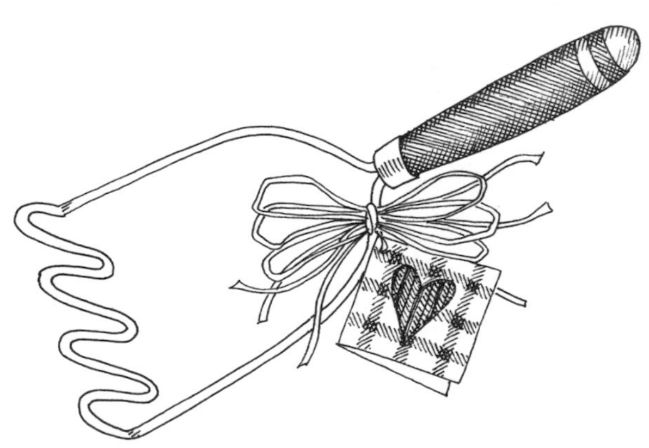

A side dish time-saver. Purchase packaged mashed potatoes at the grocery store. Heat up, blend in sour cream and cream cheese to taste, then heat up again until well blended...so yummy!

Beef de Roma

Diane Hime
Corinth, NY

I love this recipe because it's so quick & easy, but tastes like I spent all day in the kitchen!

1 lb. ground beef
1/2 c. onion, chopped
1/4 c. green pepper, chopped
1 clove garlic, minced
1 t. salt
1 t. dried parsley
1/2 t. dried oregano
1/2 t. dried basil
1/4 t. pepper
2 8-oz. cans tomato sauce
3 c. prepared rice
16-oz. container cottage cheese
Garnish: grated Parmesan cheese

Brown meat in a skillet; drain. Add onion, pepper, garlic, seasonings and tomato sauce; simmer 5 minutes. Layer rice, cottage cheese and meat mixture in a greased 3-quart casserole dish. Bake at 350 degrees for 30 minutes. Sprinkle with Parmesan cheese and bake 10 minutes or until golden. Serves 4 to 6.

As soon as a baking dish is empty, submerge it in hot, soapy water to speed clean-up...saves oodles of scrubbing time!

Mexicalli Pie

Carol Huck
Chester, NJ

A side of refried beans or Spanish rice will complete this dinner nicely.

1 lb. ground beef
1/2 c. onion, chopped
1/2 c. green pepper, chopped
1-1/2 c. frozen corn, thawed and drained
1 c. chunky salsa
3/4 c. shredded Cheddar cheese
1/8 t. pepper
1 c. corn chips, crushed

Brown meat, onion and pepper in a skillet; drain. Add corn, salsa, Cheddar cheese and pepper. Spray a 10" pie plate with non-stick vegetable spray. Place meat mixture in pie plate; top with crushed chips. Bake at 350 degrees for 30 minutes. Let cool for 10 minutes. Serves 6 to 8.

Stir up some simple artichoke salsa to spoon over casserole dishes! Drain and finely chop one, 6-ounce jar of marinated artichoke hearts and blend with one finely chopped chile pepper, one minced garlic clove and the juice of one lime. Delicious!

Creamy Taco Casserole

Cathy Wolf
Canton, TX

You can prepare this ahead of time and freeze it to let the flavors mingle...just don't add the evaporated milk. When you're ready to bake it, let the casserole thaw, add the milk and bake.

3 lbs. ground beef
1 onion, chopped
salt and pepper to taste
15-oz. can tomato sauce
4-1/2 oz. can chopped green chiles
2 10-oz. cans tomatoes with chiles
1 c. hot pepper sauce
16 corn tortillas, torn into large pieces and divided
3 16-oz. pkgs. pasteurized processed cheese spread, sliced and divided
12-oz. can evaporated milk
Garnish: tortilla chips, additional hot sauce

Brown ground beef with onion in a large skillet; sprinkle with salt and pepper. Drain; add tomato sauce, chiles, tomatoes with chiles and hot pepper sauce. Reduce heat to low and simmer for 20 minutes. Layer half of the tortillas, half of meat mixture and half of cheese in an ungreased jelly-roll pan sprayed with non-stick vegetable spray, pressing after each layer to pack. Repeat layers, reserving a little meat mixture to sprinkle over last cheese layer. Poke holes in the layers with a fork; pour evaporated milk over top. Allow milk to soak into casserole. Bake, uncovered, at 350 degrees for 40 to 45 minutes. Serve with chips and additional hot pepper sauce. Serves 10 to 12.

Over the weekend, prepare the week's salads ahead of time so tonight's dinner is quick & easy! Store salad in a slightly damp plastic zipping bag and refrigerate; it will be fresh for up to 4 days.

Gourmet Beef-Noodle Casserole

Michelle Greeley
Hayes, VA

While visiting my mother, I came across this recipe she had received from a friend while both were stationed in Germany in the early 1970's. Since finding this "long lost recipe" I've made it many times for my family.

1 lb. ground beef
14-1/2 oz. can diced tomatoes
8-oz. can tomato sauce
1/2 c. green pepper, chopped
4-oz. can sliced mushrooms, drained
1 clove garlic, chopped
2 t. salt
2 t. sugar
1/2 c. burgundy wine or beef broth
8-oz. pkg. cream cheese, softened
1 c. sour cream
1/3 c. onion, chopped
2 c. shredded Cheddar cheese, divided
8-oz. pkg. wide egg noodles, cooked

Brown ground beef in a skillet; drain. Add tomatoes, sauce, green pepper, mushrooms, garlic, salt, sugar and wine or broth; cover and simmer over low heat for 10 minutes. In a medium bowl, blend cream cheese, sour cream, onion and one cup Cheddar cheese; set aside. In an ungreased 13"x9" baking pan, layer half the beef mixture, half the noodles and half the cheese mixture; repeat layers. Top with remaining Cheddar cheese. Bake, uncovered, at 350 degrees for 40 minutes. Serves 6 to 8.

Serve roasted corn on the cob with dinner...ready in only 4 minutes! Place husked ears of corn under a broiler until golden on all sides.

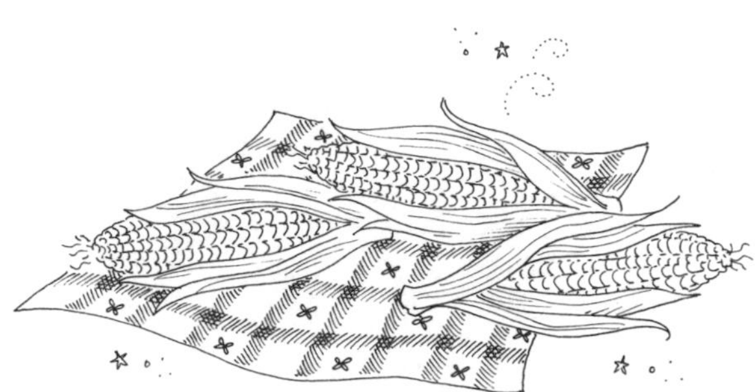

Beef

Beefy Spinach Casserole

Bec Popovich
Gooseberry Patch

A favorite at any carry-in or potluck.

1 lb. ground beef
10-oz. pkg. frozen chopped spinach, thawed and drained
1 clove garlic, minced
salt and pepper to taste
16-oz. pkg. wide egg noodles, uncooked
10-3/4 oz. can cream of mushroom soup
2-1/2 c. milk
1 c. American cheese, shredded

Brown beef in a skillet over medium heat; drain. Add spinach, garlic, salt and pepper; cook until heated through. Stir in egg noodles; spoon into a greased 13"x9" baking pan and set aside. Combine soup and milk; mix well to blend and stir gently into beef mixture. Sprinkle with cheese. Bake at 325 degrees for 45 minutes, until bubbly. Serves 8.

Cupcakes for dessert tonight? Frost them quickly by dipping in frosting rather than using a spatula.

Soft Taco Casserole

Kathy Goscha
Topeka, KS

Use flour tortillas instead of corn if you'd like.

1 lb. ground beef, browned and drained
10-3/4 oz. can tomato soup
1 c. salsa
1/2 c. milk
8-1/2 oz. can peas & carrots, drained
7 6-inch corn tortillas, cut into 1-inch squares
1-1/2 t. chili powder
1 c. shredded Cheddar cheese, divided

Combine all ingredients except 1/2 cup cheese; spread in a 2-quart casserole dish sprayed with non-stick vegetable spray. Cover and bake at 400 degrees for 30 minutes, or until hot. Sprinkle with remaining cheese; let stand until cheese melts. Makes 4 servings.

Tie together 3 pillar candles with a length of sparkly ribbon...a centerpiece in seconds.

Chiluppi

Kae Carlson
Omaha, NE

Toasted tortilla strips make this casserole different...it's gone in no time at all.

1/4 c. onion, chopped
1/4 c. green pepper, chopped
1 T. oil
1 lb. ground beef
4 t. chili powder
1 t. ground cumin
1-1/2 t. salt
3 T. all-purpose flour
8-oz. can tomato sauce
12 6-inch flour tortillas, cut into 1/2-inch strips
2 c. shredded Cheddar cheese, divided
10-3/4 oz. can Cheddar cheese soup
1/2 c. milk

In a skillet over medium heat, sauté onion and pepper in oil until transparent; add beef. Cook until beef is browned; drain. Add chili powder, cumin, salt and flour; stir well. Mix in tomato sauce and enough water to cover mixture; simmer over low heat for 30 minutes. Set aside. Toast tortilla strips on a baking sheet in the oven at 350 degrees for 3 to 4 minutes; layer half in a greased 13"x9" baking pan. Top with half of meat mixture. Sprinkle with one cup cheese; add remaining tortilla strips. Top with remaining meat mixture; set aside. Blend soup and milk together; pour over top of meat mixture. Sprinkle with remaining cheese; bake at 300 degrees for 30 to 40 minutes. Let stand 15 minutes before serving. Serves 6 to 8.

Tag sale ceramics are sweet for serving up cookies for dessert. Cleverly dress them up with some dime-store treasures...baubles, beads, even seashells! Be sure to hand wash.

Oven Beef Stew

Alice Monaghan
St. Joseph, MO

Shared with me by a good friend, this is a lifesaver on busy days. I just pop it in the oven and finish up my to-do list!

1-1/2 lbs. stew beef, cubed
5 carrots, peeled and sliced
1 c. celery, chopped
2 onions, sliced
1 potato, peeled and chopped
28-oz. can stewed tomatoes
1/2 c. fresh bread crumbs
2 t. salt
3 T. instant tapioca, uncooked

Place beef, carrots, celery, onions and potato in a bowl. Combine remaining ingredients and add to beef mixture; blend well. Place into a greased 2-1/2 quart casserole dish. Cover and bake at 250 degrees for 5 hours. Makes 6 servings.

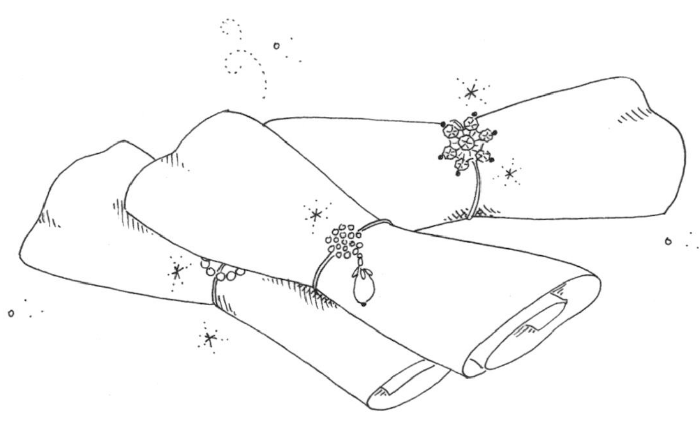

Bits of vintage jewelry and faux flowers really dress up a plain napkin. Slide pint-size trinkets over metallic silver or gold thread, then tie on.

Beef

Beefy Noodle Bake

Samantha Starks
Madison, WI

Golden, melted cheese and wide egg noodles...what a combination.

1 lb. ground beef
10-3/4 oz. can tomato soup
10-3/4 oz. can vegetable soup
salt and pepper to taste
8-oz. pkg. wide egg noodles, cooked
8 slices American cheese

Brown beef in a large skillet over medium heat; drain. Add soups, salt and pepper; stir in noodles and simmer over low heat for 10 minutes. Pour into an ungreased 11"x7" baking pan; top with cheese slices. Bake at 350 degrees for 20 minutes, until cheese is melted and golden. Makes 8 servings.

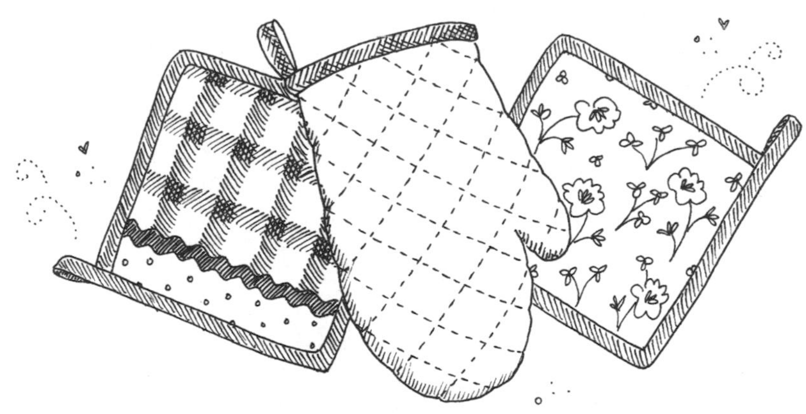

Give instant charm to "too perfect" tablecloths, fabric or silk flowers. Make a strong brew of tea or coffee and use it to dip or brush on the piece. Repeat, depending on how much character you want to give something that feels too new.

Easy Weeknight Favorite

Sherry Gordon
Arlington Heights, IL

Bakes in only 25 minutes, this can be baking away while the salad and side dishes are being prepared.

1-1/2 lbs. ground beef
14-1/2 oz. can diced tomatoes
1 t. salt
1 T. sugar
1-1/2 c. sour cream
3-oz. pkg. cream cheese, softened
1/4 c. onion, chopped
8-oz. pkg. medium egg noodles, cooked
1 c. shredded Cheddar cheese

Brown beef in a large skillet over medium heat; drain. Add tomatoes, salt and sugar; reduce to low heat and simmer for 15 minutes. Set aside. Combine sour cream, cream cheese and onion in a bowl; mix well and set aside. Place half the noodles in a lightly greased 13"x9" baking pan; top with meat mixture, then sour cream mixture. Layer remaining noodles over top; sprinkle with cheese. Bake at 350 degrees for 25 minutes. Serves 6.

Don't store tomatoes in the refrigerator, they'll quickly lose their "just-picked" taste. Keep them on a pantry shelf instead.

Salisbury Steak with Potatoes

Alisha Walker
Eagar, AZ

This is a favorite dish I love to serve with garden-fresh corn-on-the- cob...delicious!

4 potatoes, peeled and sliced
1-1/2 lbs. ground beef
1 c. bread crumbs
1 egg, beaten
1 onion, chopped
26-oz. can cream of mushroom soup
1 1/2-oz. pkg. beefy onion soup mix

Arrange potatoes in the bottom of a lightly greased 13"x9" baking pan. Combine ground beef, bread crumbs, egg and onion; form into 6 patties. Place patties on top of potato slices. Combine soup and dry soup mix; blend well. Pour over patties and potatoes. Bake at 350 degrees for 1-1/2 hours. Serves 6.

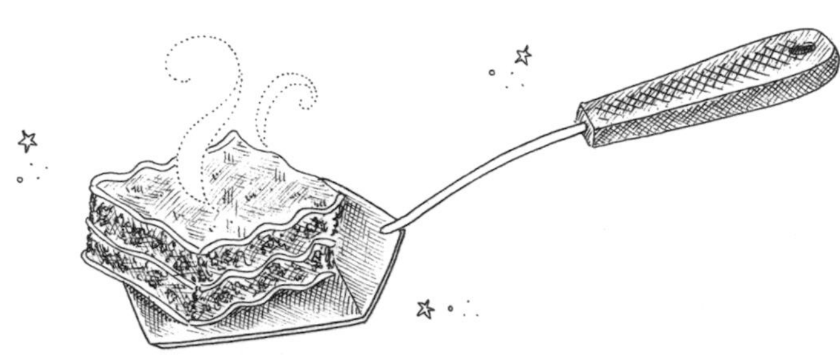

To avoid scratching non-stick baking pans, be sure to serve up casseroles using plastic or wood spatulas, never metal.

Layered Southwestern Bake

Laura Fuller
Fort Wayne, IN

Everyone's favorites all rolled into one casserole!

1 lb. ground beef
2 onions, chopped
1 green pepper, chopped
1/4 c. frozen green peas
1/2 t. chili powder
1/2 t. red pepper flakes
14-1/2 oz. can tomatoes,
drained and diced
1/4 c. tomato paste
15-1/4 oz. can kidney beans,
drained and rinsed
11-oz. can corn, drained
4 6-inch corn tortillas,
quartered
1/3 c. shredded Cheddar cheese

Combine beef, onions and pepper in a large skillet; cook over medium heat until beef is browned and onions are tender. Drain. Add peas; sprinkle with chili powder and red pepper flakes. Stir in tomatoes and tomato paste; reduce heat to low and simmer for 5 minutes. Add beans and corn; stir to combine. Spoon half the mixture into a greased 11"x7" baking pan; top with half the tortilla quarters. Layer with remaining beef mixture. Cover and bake at 350 degrees for 25 minutes; remove cover and top with remaining tortillas and cheese. Bake an additional 10 minutes or until cheese is melted. Serves 4 to 6.

Zip up an everyday salad by tossing in some finely chopped apples, raisins and walnut pieces. Add edible flowers too! Pesticide-free chive blossoms, nasturtiums and violets are all perfectly edible.

Oriental Beef & Rice

Tami Meyer
Plant City, FL

Spread a little Chinese mustard on individual servings for a tangy surprise.

1 lb. ground beef
1 onion, chopped
salt and pepper to taste
1 c. instant rice, uncooked
10-3/4 oz. can cream of mushroom soup
10-3/4 oz. can cream of chicken soup
1 c. warm water
1/4 c. soy sauce

Combine beef, onion, salt and pepper in a skillet; cook over medium heat until beef is browned and onion is tender. Drain; set aside. Mix rice, soups, water and soy sauce together; stir in beef mixture. Spoon into a lightly greased 13"x9" baking pan; bake at 350 degrees for 50 minutes. Serves 4 to 6.

To keep rice from becoming sticky, don't stir it after cooking, instead, gently fluff it with a fork. It works every time!

Western Round-Up

Kay Marone
Des Moines, IA

Zesty flavors topped with a cornbread crust...yum!

1 lb. ground beef
2 red peppers, cut into 2-inch squares
1/4 c. onion, chopped
15-oz. can baked beans
1 T. fajita seasoning
8-1/2 oz. pkg. cornbread mix
1 egg
1/3 c. milk

Combine ground beef, peppers and onion in a large oven-safe skillet over medium-high heat; heat and stir until beef is browned and onion is translucent. Drain. Add beans and fajita seasoning; heat through, stirring frequently. Spread out evenly in skillet; set aside. Mix cornbread with egg and milk according to package directions. Spread evenly over ground beef mixture in skillet; place skillet in the oven. Bake at 350 degrees for 20 minutes, or until a toothpick inserted into cornbread layer comes out clean. Let cool slightly before serving; cut into wedges. Serves 6.

A big, home-baked cookie makes a sweet after-dinner treat. Place each in a cellophane bag tied closed with a ribbon. Family & friends will feel extra special!

Tamale Pie

Brenda Derby
Northborough, MA

Kids will love this...adults too!

1 onion, chopped
1 clove garlic, minced
1 T. oil
1-1/2 lbs. ground beef
8-oz. pkg. corn chips, crushed
15-1/4 oz. can corn, drained
14-3/4 oz. can creamed corn
4-oz. can black olives, drained and chopped
2 8-oz. cans tomato sauce, divided
2 T. chili powder
1/8 t. cayenne pepper

Sauté onion and garlic in oil in a skillet just until soft; add ground beef and heat until beef loses its pink color. Add corn chips, corn, creamed corn, olives, one can tomato sauce and seasonings to meat mixture; mix well and pour into an ungreased 13"x9" baking pan. Top with remaining tomato sauce. Cover and bake 45 minutes at 350 degrees. Makes 6 to 8 servings.

Do the unexpected at dinnertime! Line a sombrero with bandannas and fill with tortilla chips...perfect for munching while waiting for Tamale Pie to bake.

Souper Meat & Potatoes Pie

Ann Fehr
Trappe, PA

For me, this is real comfort food.

1 lb. ground beef
10-3/4 oz. can cream of mushroom soup, divided
1/4 c. onion, chopped
1 egg beaten
1/4 c. fine bread crumbs
2 T. fresh parsley
1/4 t. salt
1/8 t. pepper
2 c. potatoes, peeled, cooked and mashed
1/4 c. shredded mild Cheddar cheese

Mix beef, 1/2 cup soup, onion, egg, bread crumbs, parsley and seasonings. Press firmly into an ungreased 9" pie plate. Bake at 350 degrees for 25 minutes; drain. Layer potatoes, remaining soup and cheese. Bake an additional 10 minutes; cut into wedges to serve. Makes 4 to 6 servings.

A vintage postcard napkin ring...just color copy, wrap around a folded napkin and secure with double-sided tape.

Potato Puff Casserole

Debi DeVore
Dover, OH

Everyone loves potato puffs!

2 lbs. ground beef, browned and drained
10-3/4 oz. can cream of mushroom soup
32-oz. pkg. frozen potato puffs, thawed
Optional: shredded Cheddar cheese

Arrange ground beef in an ungreased 13"x9" baking pan. Spread soup over beef; cover with potato puffs. Sprinkle with cheese, if desired. Bake at 375 degrees for 20 to 30 minutes, until heated through. Serves 6 to 8.

Add a little food coloring to the water in a vase of flowers for a soft, pastel color.

Hamburger Pie

Faye Hood
Fort Deposit, AL

A salad alongside makes this a "must-have" dinner.

1-1/2 lbs. ground beef
5 potatoes, peeled and sliced
1 onion, sliced
10-3/4 oz. can cream of mushroom soup
10-3/4 oz. can cream of celery soup
1/2 c. water
salt and pepper to taste

Shape beef into walnut-sized balls; flatten and arrange in a lightly greased 13"x9" baking pan. Layer with potatoes; top with onion. Set aside. Combine soups and water; pour over potato mixture. Cover; bake at 375 degrees for one hour. Serves 6 to 8.

Whenever just a little onion is needed for a casserole recipe, use green onions instead. Easily cut with kitchen scissors, they add a light onion flavor with no leftover onion to store.

Pantry Casserole

Vickie

Mix a little of this, a little of that and enjoy!

1 lb. ground beef
2 t. poultry seasoning
2 t. dried thyme
1-1/2 t. ground cumin
salt and pepper to taste
2 t. garlic, minced
3 potatoes, thinly sliced
2 T. butter
1 onion, thinly sliced in rings
2 c. sliced mushrooms
10-3/4 oz. can cream of chicken soup
3/4 c. water
20 saltine crackers, crushed
Garnish: 1/8 t. paprika

Place ground beef in a large skillet; sprinkle with seasonings and garlic. Heat, stirring frequently, over medium heat until browned. Drain; transfer to an ungreased 13"x9" baking dish. Arrange 2 layers of sliced potatoes over beef mixture, sprinkling each layer with salt and pepper; set aside. Melt butter in the skillet over medium heat; sauté onion and mushrooms until crisp-tender. Spread over potatoes; set aside. Combine soup and water; spread evenly over casserole. Top with cracker crumbs and sprinkle with paprika. Cover with aluminum foil and bake for one hour, or until potatoes are soft. Remove foil and bake an additional 10 minutes, until golden. Serves 4 to 6.

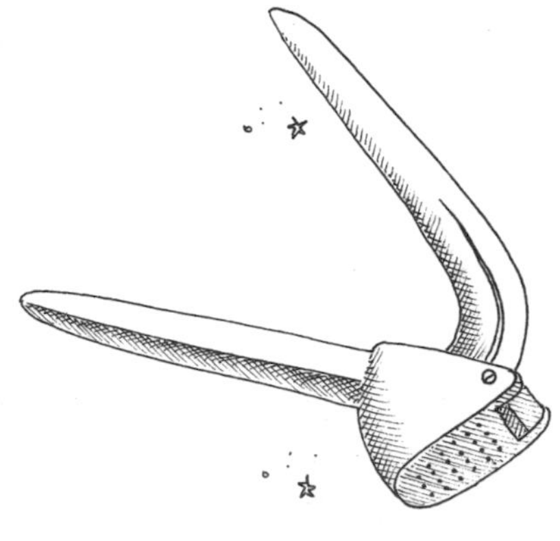

Save chopping time...use a garlic press. Don't even bother peeling the clove, just place it in the garlic press and close. The garlic paste is easily removed and ready to add to any recipe. The peel slides off and stays inside the press.

3-Bean Bake

Brenda Doak
Delaware, OH

A tasty combination...you'll get asked for this recipe!

1 lb. ground beef
6 slices bacon, diced
1 onion, chopped
1 green pepper, chopped
1 T. white vinegar
1 T. mustard
1/2 c. catsup
1/2 c. brown sugar, packed
15-oz. can kidney beans, drained and rinsed
16-oz. can chili beans
15-oz. can pork & beans
6 slices American cheese
1 c. tortilla chips, crushed

Brown ground beef, bacon, onion and pepper in a large skillet over medium-high heat; drain. Pour into an ungreased 3-quart casserole dish. Add vinegar, mustard, catsup, brown sugar and beans; mix to blend. Bake at 375 degrees for 45 to 50 minutes; remove from oven and top with cheese and chips. Bake an additional 5 to 10 minutes, until cheese is melted and bubbly. Serves 6.

To easily separate bacon slices, roll the package of bacon lengthwise and secure with a rubber band before refrigerating. When the package is unrolled, it's so easy to separate each slice!

Beef

Weekend Beef Burgundy

Virgina Watson
Scranton, PA

Try this easy dish on a Saturday or Sunday...it takes some time to bake, but it's well worth the wait!

- 2 lbs. stew beef, cubed
- 10-3/4 oz. can cream of mushroom soup
- 1/2 c. onion, chopped
- 1 t. beef bouillon granules
- 1-oz. pkg. herb and lemon soup mix, divided
- 4-1/2 oz. can sliced mushrooms, drained
- 1/2 c. Burgundy wine or beef broth
- 4 c. prepared egg noodles

Combine beef, soup, onion and bouillon in a large bowl; mix well. Stir in half the package of soup mix, reserving the rest for another recipe. Spread in a lightly greased 13"x9" baking pan; cover and bake at 325 degrees for 4 hours. Add mushrooms and wine or broth; bake for an additional 10 minutes. Add noodles and stir to combine. Serves 8 to 10.

For a quick fix to spilled wine, cover the stain with a thick layer of salt and follow with a cold water rinse. If the stain remains, blot it with liquid laundry detergent, rinse and launder.

Flemish Beef Stew

Jennie Gist
Gooseberry Patch

I've even prepared this over a campfire...every bit as delicious!

- 5 slices bacon, cut into 1/2-inch pieces
- 2 lbs. boneless beef chuck, cut into 1-inch cubes
- 2 onions, sliced
- 2 cloves garlic, minced
- 3/4 c. regular or non-alcoholic beer
- 12-oz. jar beef gravy
- 1 c. baby carrots
- 1/2 t. dried thyme
- Garnish: fresh parsley, chopped

Cook and stir bacon until crisp over medium heat in a Dutch oven. Remove bacon with a slotted spoon; set aside. Add beef to drippings; cook over medium-high heat until browned, stirring occasionally. Add onions and garlic; cook and stir for one minute. Remove from heat; stir in remaining ingredients except parsley. Cover and bake at 350 degrees for 45 minutes. Uncover and bake an additional 45 minutes. Sprinkle servings with parsley and reserved bacon. Serves 4 to 6.

Easy herbal lemonade iced tea the whole family will love. Mix a 12-ounce can of frozen lemonade concentrate with 1-1/2 cans of water. Blend into one quart of prepared herbal tea.

Unstuffed Cabbage

Diana Krol
Nickerson, KS

This dish fills my home with the aroma of soothing comfort food.

1-1/2 lbs. ground beef
1-1/2 t. salt
1/2 t. pepper
3 T. long-cooking rice, uncooked
2 t. onion, minced
2 eggs
28-oz. can diced tomatoes
6-oz. can tomato paste
1/2 c. brown sugar, packed
1/2 c. vinegar
2 t. dried onion
1 head cabbage, chopped and divided

Mix beef, salt, pepper, rice, minced onion and eggs together; form into 12, one-inch balls and set aside. In another bowl, combine tomatoes, tomato paste, sugar, vinegar and onion; set aside. Place half the cabbage in a lightly greased 13"x9" baking pan; top with half the tomato mixture. Top with meatballs; pour remaining sauce over top. Sprinkle with remaining cabbage. Cover; bake at 325 degrees for one hour. Reduce heat to 250 degrees; bake for an additional 3 hours. Serves 6 to 8.

To get richer-tasting tomato paste, pick up sun-dried tomato paste in a tube.

Baked Mostaccioli

Connie Bryant
Topeka, KS

Add mushrooms or olives too...you can't go wrong!

1 lb. ground beef
8-oz. pkg. mostaccioli pasta, cooked
30-oz. jar spaghetti sauce
3/4 c. grated Parmesan cheese, divided
8-oz. pkg. shredded mozzarella cheese
Optional: additional grated Parmesan cheese

Brown ground beef in a large skillet; drain. Stir in cooked pasta, sauce and 1/2 cup Parmesan cheese; spoon into a greased 13"x9" baking pan. Top with mozzarella and remaining Parmesan cheese. Bake for 20 minutes at 375 degrees, until heated through. If desired, sprinkle with additional Parmesan cheese. Makes 6 servings.

Just need a little something while dinner is baking? Slice up some fresh veggies and serve with this super-simple dip. Blend 1 cup sour cream, 1 cup cottage cheese, 1 packet dried vegetable soup mix and 1 finely sliced green onion.

Lazy-Day Lasagna

Tammy Delker
Ottumwa, IA

Here's what I do to keep the noodles from sliding away when lasagna is sliced...I just alternate the direction I lay the noodles!

12-oz. container cottage cheese
4 c. shredded mozzarella cheese, divided
2 eggs, beaten
1/3 c. grated Parmesan cheese
1/3 c. dried parsley
1 t. onion powder
1/2 t. dried basil
1/8 t. pepper
32-oz. jar spaghetti sauce
1 lb. ground beef, browned and drained
9 strips lasagna, uncooked
1/4 c. water

Mix together cottage cheese, 2 cups mozzarella cheese, eggs, Parmesan cheese and seasonings; set aside. Combine spaghetti sauce and beef; set aside. Spread one to 1-1/2 cups of meat mixture into an ungreased 13"x9" baking pan; layer 5 lasagna strips, half the cottage cheese mixture and 1-1/2 cups of meat mixture. Add remaining layer of lasagna; cover with remaining meat mixture. Top with remaining mozzarella cheese; pour water around the edges. Bake, covered, at 350 degrees for 45 minutes; uncover and bake for an additional 15 minutes. Serves 6 to 8.

Keep frosty pitchers of ice water or lemonade from dripping. Rub a piece of wax paper around the rim of the pitcher!

Roman Holiday

Leisa Dwyer
Roswell, NM

Take a vacation from time-consuming dinners...this recipe is a breeze to prepare.

1 onion, chopped
1/4 c. shortening
1 lb. ground beef
1 t. salt
1/8 t. pepper
2 c. prepared spaghetti, divided
14-1/2 oz. can diced tomatoes
3 c. shredded Cheddar cheese

Sauté onion in shortening; add meat, salt and pepper. Cook for 5 minutes or until meat is browned; drain and set aside. Layer one cup of spaghetti in a lightly greased 13"x9" baking pan; top with meat mixture. Layer with remaining spaghetti; pour in tomatoes. Sprinkle with cheese; cover. Bake at 350 degrees for 35 minutes; remove cover. Bake for an additional 10 minutes. Serves 6 to 8.

We'll always treasure our handed-down recipe cards handwritten by Mom or Grandma. One way to protect them from kitchen spills and smudges is by laminating them. Just buy self-laminating sheets, arrange a recipe card between 2 of the sheets, seal smoothly and trim any excess plastic from the edges.

Tamale Pot Pie

Marian Buckley
Fontana, CA

Not your "usual" pot pie filling...this will be a hit!

1 lb. ground beef
10-oz. pkg. frozen corn, thawed
14-1/2 oz. can diced tomatoes
2-1/4 oz. can sliced black olives, drained
1 c. plus 2 T. biscuit baking mix, divided
1 T. chili powder
2 t. ground cumin
1/2 t. salt
1/2 c. cornmeal
1/2 c. milk
2 T. chopped green chiles
1 egg

Cook ground beef in a large skillet over medium heat until browned; drain. Stir in corn, tomatoes with juice, olives, 2 tablespoons baking mix, chili powder, cumin and salt. Heat to boiling, stirring frequently. Boil and stir one minute. Keep warm over low heat. Stir together remaining ingredients until blended. Pour beef mixture into an ungreased 9"x9" baking pan. Spread cornmeal mixture over beef mixture. Bake at 400 degrees about 20 to 30 minutes, until crust is golden. Serves 6.

Did you know a lemon can help remove tarnish from copper pots & pans? Wrap lemon halves in cheesecloth and sprinkle coarse kosher salt over the tarnish. Rub until tarnish is gone.

Mexican Casserole

Shannon Pettus
Rowlett, TX

I like mild enchilada sauce, but you could choose a hot sauce to spice it up. I think this is the best!

12 6-inch corn tortillas, quartered
1 lb. ground beef, browned and drained
10-oz. can enchilada sauce
15-oz. can ranch-style beans
10-3/4 oz. can cream of chicken soup
2 c. shredded Cheddar cheese
14-1/2 oz. can diced tomatoes

Arrange half the tortillas in the bottom of a lightly greased 13"x9" baking pan. Place meat on top of tortillas. Mix together enchilada sauce, beans and soup; pour over meat. Sprinkle cheese on top, then add remaining tortillas. Place diced tomatoes on top. Bake at 350 degrees for 45 minutes. Makes 6 to 8 servings.

It's easy to keep a cutting board from slipping while you chop. Set it on a piece of non-slip mesh easily found at home improvement stores...it's the same kind of pad used to keep area rugs from slipping!

Deep-Dish Taco Squares

Jody Bolen
Ashland, OH

Full of flavor, but not too hot & spicy.

2 c. biscuit baking mix
1/2 c. water
1 lb. ground beef
1 green pepper, chopped
1 onion, chopped
1/8 t. garlic powder
8-oz. can tomato sauce
1-1/4 oz. pkg. taco seasoning mix
1 c. shredded Cheddar cheese
1 c. sour cream
1/3 c. mayonnaise-type salad dressing
1/4 t. paprika
Garnish: sour cream, chopped tomatoes, chopped lettuce, chopped onion

Mix biscuit baking mix and water; spread in lightly greased 13"x9" baking pan. Bake at 375 degrees for 9 minutes; remove from oven and set aside. Brown together ground beef, green pepper, onion and garlic powder; drain and stir in tomato sauce and taco seasoning. Spread mixture over crust. Stir together cheese, sour cream and salad dressing; spoon over beef mixture and sprinkle with paprika. Bake at 375 degrees for an additional 25 minutes. Cut into squares; garnish with sour cream, tomatoes, lettuce and onion. Makes 12 to 15 servings.

Small pears, apples and Jack-be-Little pumpkins make the sweetest placecards. Simply punch tags with holes, slip a ribbon though each and tie to the stem.

Beef & Potato Casserole

Robin Hil
Rochester, NY

I get more requests for this recipe than anything else I cook.

- 2 T. shortening
- 2 lbs. stew beef, cubed
- 1 onion, thinly sliced
- 1 c. water
- 10-3/4 oz. can cream of mushroom soup
- 1 c. sour cream
- 1-1/4 c. milk
- 1 t. salt
- 1/4 t. pepper
- 4 potatoes, peeled and diced
- 1 c. shredded Cheddar cheese
- 1-1/4 c. whole-grain wheat flake cereal, crushed

Melt shortening in a large skillet over high heat. Add beef and onion; cook until browned. Drain; stir in water and bring to a boil. Cover; reduce heat to low and simmer for 30 minutes. Set aside. Combine soup, sour cream, milk, salt and pepper in a medium bowl; mix well. Pour meat mixture into an ungreased 13"x9" baking dish; arrange potatoes over meat. Pour soup mixture over potatoes; sprinkle with cheese and cereal. Bake, uncovered, at 350 degrees for 1-1/2 hours. Serves 6 to 8.

When topping a casserole with bread crumbs, potato chips or cereal, place in a plastic zipping bag and seal. Roll with a heavy rolling pin until the crumbs are crushed...clean-up is a breeze!

Beef

Divine Casserole

Tiffany Brinkley
Broomfield, CO

I like this with buttery, whipped potatoes...comfort food!

1 lb. ground beef
6-oz. can tomato paste
1 t. Worcestershire sauce
1/4 t. hot pepper sauce
1/8 t. dried oregano
1 onion, chopped
1/2 c. plus 2 T. butter, melted and divided
8-oz. container small curd cottage cheese
1/2 c. sour cream
1/2 c. cream cheese, softened
8-oz. pkg. egg noodles, cooked and divided

Brown beef in a large skillet over medium heat; drain. Add tomato paste, Worcestershire sauce, hot sauce and oregano; heat through and set aside. In a separate skillet over medium heat, sauté onion until translucent in 2 tablespoons butter; place in a medium bowl. Add cottage cheese, sour cream and cream cheese; blend well and set aside. Place half the noodles in an ungreased 2-quart casserole dish. Drizzle with 1/4 cup butter; spread with cheese mixture. Toss remaining noodles with remaining butter and spread over cheese mixture. Top with meat mixture. Bake at 350 degrees for 40 minutes or until bubbly. Serves 4 to 6.

Do the unexpected! Brand new terra cotta saucers lined with tea towels make fun platters for serving bread, buns or biscuits.

Beefy Cheddar Pie

Christine Gordon
Ellsworth AFB, SD

Always a favorite family dinner when I was growing up.

2 9-inch double pie crusts, divided
1 lb. ground beef
1/4 c. onion, chopped
2 T. all-purpose flour
3/4 t. salt
1/4 t. garlic salt
1-1/4 c. plus 1 T. milk, divided
3-oz. pkg. cream cheese, softened
1 egg, beaten
10-oz. pkg. frozen chopped broccoli, cooked and drained
1/2 c. shredded Monterey Jack cheese

Place one crust in an ungreased 9" pie plate; set aside. Brown beef and onion together in a skillet over medium heat; drain. Stir in flour, salt, garlic salt, 1-1/4 cups milk and cream cheese. Cook and stir until mixture is smooth and bubbly. Add a small amount of cream cheese mixture to beaten egg; stir to blend and pour back into skillet. Cook and stir for one to 2 minutes, until thickened. Stir in broccoli. Spoon into pie crust; sprinkle with cheese and place top crust over top. Seal; cut slits in crust and brush with remaining milk. Bake at 350 degrees for 20 minutes; remove from oven and cover edges of crust with aluminum foil. Bake an additional 20 to 25 minutes. Let stand 10 minutes before serving. Makes 6 servings.

A large unfolded map makes a very clever table topper! Sure to spark conversations about places you've been and spots you'd like to visit.

Pork

Ham & Cauliflower Casserole

Darrell Lawry
Kissimmee, FL

Try substituting broccoli for cauliflower...just as delicious.

3 c. cooked ham, cubed
3 c. cauliflower flowerets, cooked
1-1/2 c. sliced mushrooms
salt and pepper to taste
2 T. butter
2 T. all-purpose flour
1 c. milk
1/2 c. sour cream
1 c. shredded Cheddar cheese
1 T. dry bread crumbs

Combine ham, cauliflower and mushrooms in an ungreased 3-quart casserole dish. Sprinkle with salt and pepper and set aside. Melt butter in a saucepan; stir in flour and milk. Cook over medium heat, stirring frequently, until thickened. Stir in sour cream and cheese; continue cooking until cheese has melted and sauce is smooth. Set aside; pour sauce over top of ham mixture. Sprinkle with bread crumbs. Bake at 350 degrees for 30 to 40 minutes or until heated through. Serves 6.

Serve up fresh veggies on seaside skewers...a whimsical summertime surprise. Purchase assorted shells from a crafts store; wash well, then glue onto wooden skewers. Slide on cherry tomatoes, cucumber slices, mushrooms and cheese cubes along with a variety of sauces for dipping.

Pot O' Gold Pork Chops

Kim Hood
Beaumont, TX

This all-time family favorite recipe was passed on to me by my mother-in-law.

4 pork chops
1 T. oil
2 T. onion, chopped
2 T. butter
1 t. salt
2 T. all-purpose flour
1 c. sour cream
2 15-1/4 oz. cans corn, drained
1/2 lb. bacon, crisply cooked and crumbled
2 T. green pepper, chopped
1 T. pimento, chopped

Sprinkle pork chops with salt and pepper. Heat oil in a skillet; brown chops on both sides. Remove from skillet; set aside. Sauté onion in butter until translucent; blend in salt and flour. Stir in sour cream until smooth; add corn, bacon, pimento and pepper. Spoon into a greased 13"x9" baking pan; top with pork chops. Bake at 350 degrees for 45 minutes. Serves 4.

Whip up mix & match napkin rings from ribbon scraps...so simple. For each ring, fold a 6-inch length of ribbon in half, right sides facing, and sew ends together with a 1/4-inch seam allowance. Turn the rings right side out, and slip them around rolled napkins.

Sausage & Rice Casserole

Patricia Allen
Pasadena, TX

A homestyle casserole that's sure to satisfy.

1 lb. ground sausage
1 c. celery, diced
1/2 c. onion, chopped
1 c. long-grain rice, uncooked
14-oz. can chicken broth

Brown together sausage, celery and onion until sausage is no longer pink; drain. Combine with rice and broth in a greased 13"x9" baking pan; cover with aluminum foil. Bake at 350 degrees for one hour. Serves 4 to 6.

Save room for dessert! Keep scoops of ice cream on hand...quick & easy. Cover a baking sheet in plastic wrap and then begin scooping. Place the baking sheet back in the freezer and when it's dessert time, just add to cones or bowls.

Hashbrown-Pork Chop Casserole

Shirley Flanagan
Wooster, OH

Tender pork chops in a creamy sauce. This tastes terrific!

5 pork chops
1 T. oil
1 c. sour cream
10-3/4 oz. can cream of celery soup
1/2 c. milk
32-oz. pkg. frozen shredded hashbrowns, thawed
1 c. onion, chopped
1 c. shredded Cheddar cheese

In a large skillet over medium heat, brown pork chops on both sides in oil. Set aside. Combine sour cream, soup and milk in a large bowl; add hashbrowns and onion; stir to coat. Spread in an ungreased 13"x9" baking pan and sprinkle with cheese. Top with pork chops. Bake at 375 degrees for 45 to 50 minutes, until heated through and pork chops are fully cooked. Serves 5.

Why wait for a huge pot of water to boil? Steam fresh ears of corn in just minutes. Bring 2 inches of water in a stockpot to a boil, then stand ears stem-sides down in the pot. Cover and steam until tender, about 6 to 8 minutes.

Hunter's Stew

Leah Finks
Gooseberry Patch

This recipe was created when my mom and I began searching the pantry and went "hunting" for ingredients to create something new!

7-oz. pkg. macaroni & cheese, uncooked
10-oz. pkg. frozen peas & carrots
4-oz. can mushrooms, drained
2 c. cooked ham, cubed
1 onion, chopped

In an ungreased 2-quart casserole dish, combine dry macaroni with cheese packet. Add butter and milk as directed on the package. Stir in remaining ingredients. Bake at 350 degrees for 35 to 40 minutes. Serves 4.

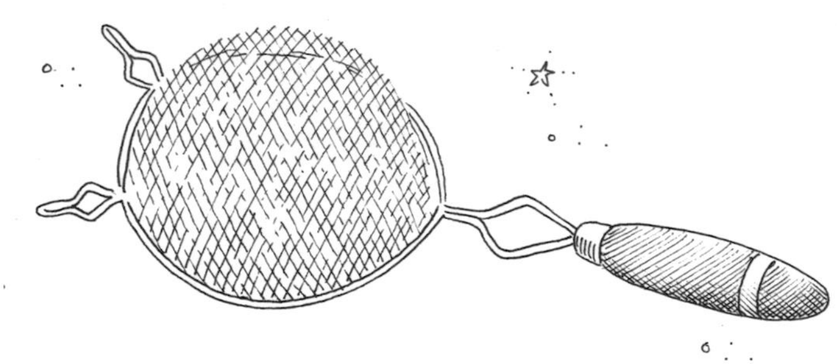

Browning meat for a casserole dish? Often it can spatter, so if there's no spatter guard handy, a large sieve can do the job...just place it face down over the food cooking in the pan.

Kielbasa Mac & Cheese

Tammy Rogers
Gordonsville, VA

So easy to make...whip it up for any weeknight dinner.

7-oz. pkg. macaroni and cheese, cooked
1 lb. Kielbasa sausage, sliced
10-3/4 oz. can cream of chicken soup
1/3 c. milk
2 c. shredded Cheddar cheese, divided
Optional: dried parsley or cayenne pepper to taste

Prepare macaroni and cheese according to package directions. In a large mixing bowl, combine sausage, prepared macaroni and cheese, soup, milk and half the Cheddar cheese. Mix well; pour into a greased 1-1/2 quart casserole dish. Top with remaining cheese, sprinkle with parsley or cayenne pepper, if desired. Bake at 350 degrees for approximately 30 minutes, or until heated through. Serves 4 to 6.

When whisking together ingredients in a bowl, a damp kitchen towel can keep the bowl in place. Just twist the towel securely around the base of the bowl.

Apple-Stuffed Pork Chops

Harriett Moorman
Aurora, TX

A scrumptious way to serve pork chops. So easy to make, but it looks like you spent hours in the kitchen!

- 6 thick pork chops
- salt and pepper to taste
- 1-1/2 c. toasted bread crumbs
- 1/2 c. apple, cored and chopped
- 1/2 c. shredded sharp Cheddar cheese
- 2 T. raisins
- 2 T. butter, melted
- 2 T. orange juice
- 1/4 t. salt
- 1/8 t. cinnamon

Cut a pocket into the side of each pork chop; sprinkle pockets with salt and pepper. Set aside. Toss bread crumbs, apple, cheese and raisins together; set aside. Combine butter, orange juice, salt and cinnamon; stir into apple mixture. Stuff pockets with mixture; place in an ungreased 13"x9" baking pan. Bake, uncovered, at 350 degrees for 15 minutes; cover. Bake for an additional 15 minutes. Makes 6 servings.

When the spoon rest is out of reach, try this quick fix to keep the spoon from sliding into the stockpot. Simply clip a wooden clothespin to the spoon handle so it catches on the rim of the pot!

Blue Ribbon Ham Casserole

Laura Jones
Louisville, KY

A tried & true county fair blue-ribbon winner!

1-1/2 lbs. yams, boiled, peeled and sliced 3/4-inch thick
2 c. cooked ham, chopped
1-1/2 c. Golden Delicious apples, peeled, cored and sliced
1/4 t. salt
1/4 t. paprika
1/2 c. brown sugar, packed
2 T. bourbon or apple juice
2 T. butter

Arrange half the yams in a greased 2-quart round casserole dish; set aside. Layer ham evenly over yams, then layer apples evenly over ham. Arrange remaining yams over the apples; sprinkle with salt and paprika. Set aside. Combine brown sugar and bourbon or apple juice; sprinkle evenly over ingredients in baking dish. Dot with butter. Bake, covered, for 20 minutes. Baste with pan juices; bake, uncovered, for an additional 25 minutes. Baste and serve. Makes 6 servings.

When grilling kabobs to serve alongside dinner, it's easy to keep the veggies from slipping off...spear them on 2 skewers instead of one.

Cheesy Spinach & Sausage Bake

Rhonda Reeder
Ellicott City, MD

A rich-tasting blend of cheese and sausage.

1 lb. ground Italian sausage
8-oz. can tomato sauce
10-oz. pkg. frozen chopped spinach, thawed and drained
2 c. cottage cheese
1/2 c. grated Parmesan cheese
1 egg, beaten
2 c. shredded mozzarella cheese

Brown sausage in a large skillet over medium heat; stir in tomato sauce and heat through. Set aside. Combine spinach, cottage cheese, Parmesan cheese and egg in a large bowl. Mix well and spread into a lightly greased 13"x9" baking pan. Spoon sausage mixture over spinach mixture and top with mozzarella cheese. Bake at 350 degrees for 40 minutes. Serves 8.

"Brew" some refreshing herbal tea without even boiling water! Fill a glass jar or pitcher with cold water and a few bags of favorite tea; let steep in the refrigerator overnight. Remove the teabags and enjoy!

Oven-Baked Ragout

Nancy Wise
Little Rock, AR

Shared with me by a friend who can always "whip up" a wonderful meal.

2 to 2-1/2 lbs. boneless pork, cubed
2 T. oil
1/4 c. all-purpose flour
13-3/4 oz. can chicken broth
1-1/4 c. white wine or chicken broth, divided
3 T. dried, minced onion
1/2 t. seasoned salt
1/2 t. dried, minced garlic
1/2 t. dried rosemary
1/4 t. pepper
1/4 t. dried thyme
1/4 t. dried marjoram
2 c. carrots, peeled and sliced
10-oz. pkg. frozen peas, thawed
6 slices bacon
2 c. sliced mushrooms
Garnish: dried parsley

Brown pork on all sides, one-third at a time, in hot oil in a Dutch oven; remove and set aside. Add flour to Dutch oven; cook over medium heat, stirring and scraping bottom of pan, for 2 minutes. Stir in chicken broth, one cup wine or broth and seasonings. Cook, stirring constantly, until mixture boils and thickens. Remove from heat; stir in browned pork. Cover Dutch oven and bake at 325 degrees for 1-1/2 hours. Stir in carrots and peas; bake, covered, an additional 30 minutes or until carrots are tender. Fry bacon in large skillet until crisp; remove, crumble and set aside. Drain, leaving 3 tablespoons drippings in skillet; sauté mushrooms about 3 minutes. Add remaining wine or broth; simmer 3 to 5 minutes. Stir mushroom mixture into Dutch oven. Garnish with reserved bacon and parsley. Serves 6 to 8.

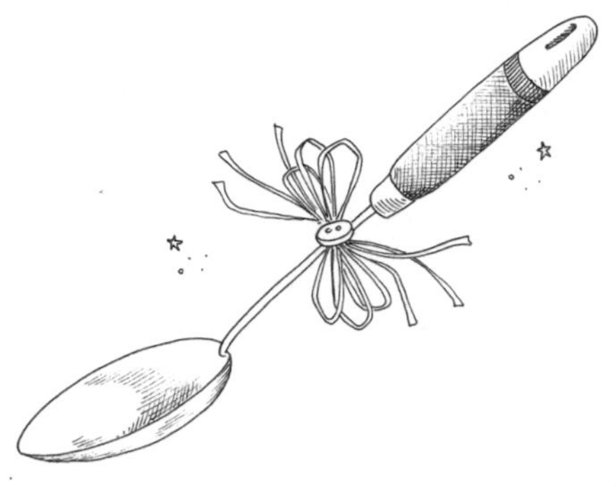

Instead of tossing the wrapper after you've used a stick of butter, store it in the freezer inside a plastic zipping bag. When it's time to butter a baking dish, take out a wrapper, let it soften slightly and use.

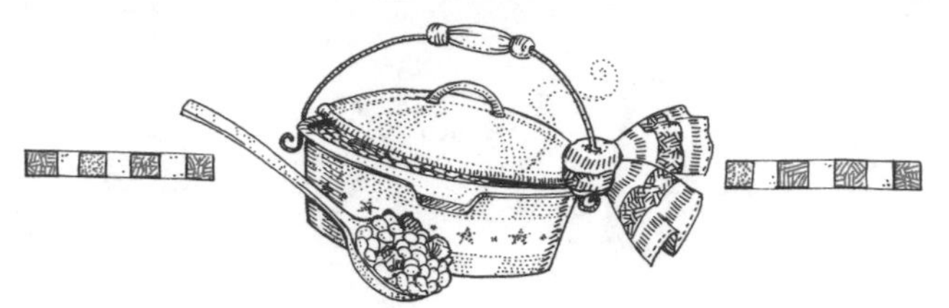

Scalloped Cabbage & Ham

Nola Coons
Gooseberry Patch

Ideal for potlucks or carry-ins. You can even substitute a bag of coleslaw mix for the chopped cabbage. How easy!

1 head cabbage, chopped
1 onion, chopped
1-1/2 c. cooked ham, diced
4 T. butter, divided
2 T. all-purpose flour
1 c. milk
3/4 c. American cheese, cubed
1 t. salt
2 T. dry bread crumbs

Steam cabbage and onion in a small amount of water until crisp-tender. Add ham and place in a greased 11"x7" baking pan; set aside. Melt 2 tablespoons butter in a skillet over low heat; stir in flour and milk until smooth. Add cheese and salt; stir until cheese is melted. Pour over cabbage mixture; sprinkle with bread crumbs and dot with remaining butter. Bake at 300 degrees for 30 minutes. Serves 4.

Colorful wallpaper scraps can work magic on serving trays...and keep cups or plates from sliding around. Give the paper a little zip by using decorative-edge scissors to trim it to fit the tray.

Sweet Potato Bake

Rebekah Burns
Ridgway, PA

The sausage in this recipe adds a different taste to the combination of sweet potatoes and apples. We always double this recipe!

- 2 sweet potatoes, peeled and sliced
- 3 apples, cored, peeled and sliced
- 1 lb. ground sausage, browned and drained
- 2 T. sugar
- 1 T. all-purpose flour
- 1/4 t. cinnamon
- 1/4 t. salt
- 1/2 c. water

Arrange sweet potatoes, apples and sausage in a greased 2-quart casserole dish. Combine remaining ingredients; spoon over top. Cover and bake at 375 degrees for 50 to 60 minutes, or until sweet potatoes and apples are tender. Makes 4 to 6 servings.

Here's an easy way to help everyone keep track of their own beverage glass...give each glass a name tag. Make tags out of construction paper with a shaped paper punch, available at crafts stores. Write names on tags, and use a hole punch to make small holes. Thread wired ribbon through the holes, then secure to the glass stems.

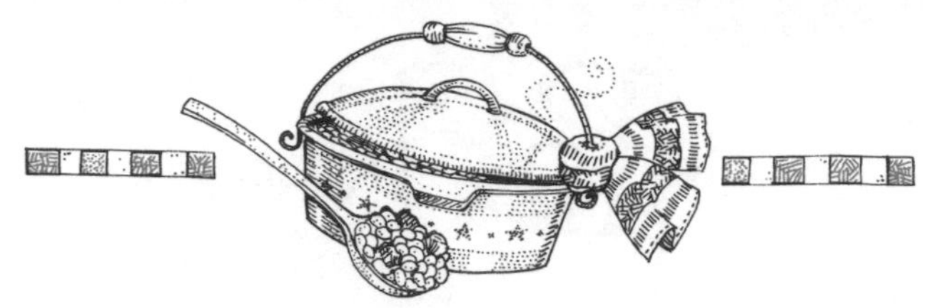

Ham-Swiss Ring-Around

Linda Catron
Galax, VA

This makes a pretty presentation.

5-oz. can ham
1 c. shredded Swiss cheese
1/2 c. butter, melted
10-oz. pkg. frozen broccoli, cooked
1 T. mustard
1/2 c. onion, chopped
8-oz. tube refrigerated crescent rolls
Garnish: grated Parmesan cheese

Combine ham, cheese, butter, broccoli, mustard and onion in bowl; set aside. On an ungreased 12" round pizza pan, unroll crescent rolls so flat sides makes a circle with the points outward. Spoon ham mixture onto rolls. Fold in crescent roll points and tuck ends in. Sprinkle with Parmesan cheese. Bake at 350 degrees for 20 to 25 minutes, or until golden. Serves 4 to 6.

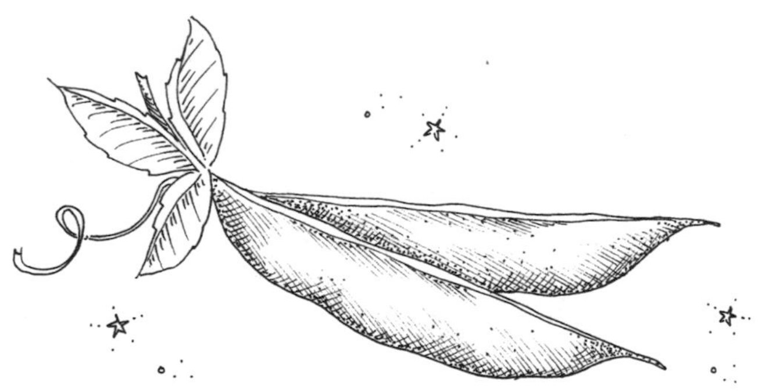

Garden-fresh green beans make a super side dish and it's a snap to keep them colorful and crisp. After boiling and draining, transfer to a colander. Dunk them, still in the colander, in a large bowl of ice water. Lift the colander after a minute, and they'll be ready to eat.

Pork Chop Bake

Jennifer Best
Hesperia, CA

My mother-in-law says you have to serve apples with pork. So I place some frozen strawberries in the microwave for a few seconds until they are soft. Then I blend them into applesauce...yummy!

1 T. oil
4 to 6 pork chops
10-3/4 oz. can cream of mushroom with roasted garlic soup
1 c. sour cream
1/4 c. milk
3 stalks celery, chopped
1/8 t. paprika
4 c. redskin potatoes, sliced
salt and pepper to taste
Optional: dried parsley, paprika

Heat oil in a large skillet; add chops and heat until golden on both sides. Remove from skillet and set aside. Mix together soup, sour cream, milk, celery and paprika; set aside. Arrange potatoes in a lightly greased 13"x9" baking pan. Pour soup mixture over potatoes. Arrange pork chops on top of soup; press down into soup, leaving tops exposed. Add salt and pepper to taste; sprinkle with parsley and paprika, if desired. Cover and bake for 1-1/4 hours at 375 degrees. Makes 4 to 6 servings.

Giant ice cubes! Add layers of thinly sliced lemons, limes and oranges in muffin cups. Fill each cup halfway with water and freeze. So pretty floating in a pitcher of tea, lemonade or ice water.

Italian Lasagna

John Alexander
New Britain, CT

Always a hit for Sunday dinner, and there's just enough time to toss a fresh salad while waiting to cut the lasagna into servings.

1 lb. ground Italian sausage
1 clove garlic, minced
1 T. fresh basil
1 T. dried oregano
2 t. salt, divided
32-oz. can whole tomatoes, chopped
2 6-oz. cans tomato paste
2 eggs, beaten
3 c. cottage cheese
1/2 c. grated Parmesan cheese
1/2 t. pepper
10-oz. pkg. lasagna, cooked
16-oz. pkg. shredded mozzarella cheese, divided

Brown Italian sausage in a large saucepan; drain. Add garlic, basil, oregano, 1-1/2 teaspoons salt and tomatoes. Simmer, uncovered, 30 minutes, stirring occasionally. Set aside. Blend together eggs, cottage cheese, Parmesan cheese, remaining salt and pepper. Set aside. Layer half the prepared lasagna in a lightly greased 13"x9" baking pan; spread with half the cottage cheese mixture. Add half the mozzarella and half the meat sauce. Repeat layering. Bake at 350 degrees for 45 minutes. Let stand 15 minutes before serving. Serves 8.

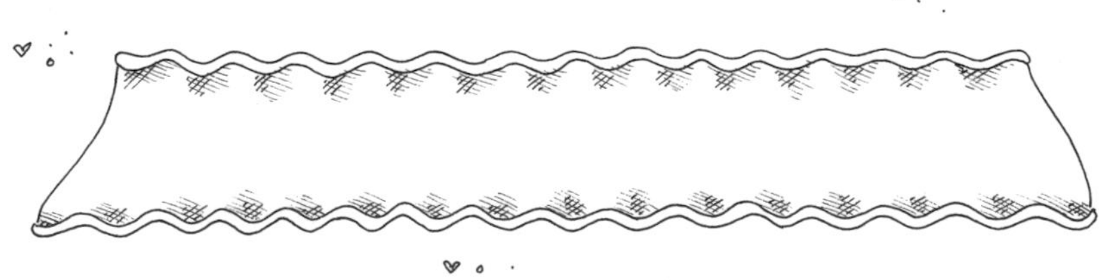

Noodles are not only amusing, but delicious.
-Julia Child

Pasta di Carla

Carla Urse
Columbus, OH

I threw this together one night and everyone loved it! It's great the next day for lunch too, if your family is small...if not, you won't have to worry about leftovers!

1 lb. ground Italian sausage
1 green pepper, chopped
1 red pepper, chopped
1 onion, chopped
2 14-1/2 oz. cans diced tomatoes with Italian seasoning
8-oz. pkg. sliced mushrooms
16-oz. pkg. rigatoni pasta, cooked
26-oz. jar spaghetti sauce
3 c. shredded mozzarella cheese, divided
Italian seasoning to taste

Brown sausage in a large skillet over medium heat. Add peppers and onion and sauté until tender; drain. Add tomatoes and mushrooms; simmer until heated through. Combine sausage mixture with rigatoni and spaghetti sauce; mix well to coat pasta. Add 2-1/2 cups mozzarella; sprinkle with Italian seasoning. Stir to blend; pour into an ungreased 13"x9" baking pan. Bakc at 350 degrees for 20 to 25 minutes, until heated through and cheese is melted. Serve in bowls; sprinkle with remaining mozzarella to taste. Serves 6 to 8.

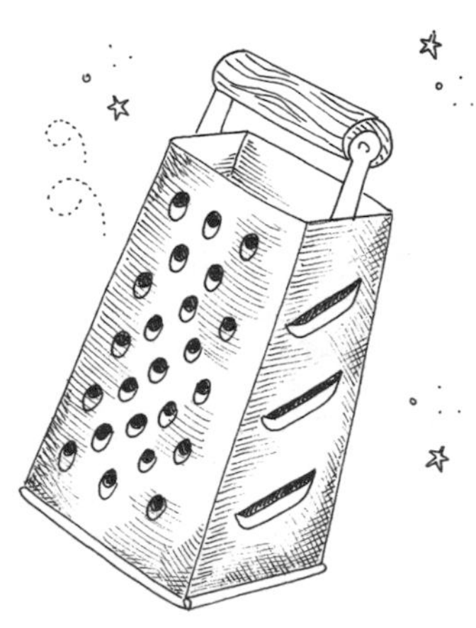

Fresh mozzarella is delicious on casserole dishes but can be difficult to grate. Freeze it first! Wrap a block of mozzarella in plastic wrap, and freeze for 20 minutes; then grate. Store the grated cheese in a resealable plastic zipping bag in the refrigerator for up to 5 days.

Party Ham Casserole

Jill Williams
Hiawatha, KS

This is the best casserole I have ever made...my whole family loves it. It's quick, easy and when I serve it with a fruit salad, I have a complete meal in no time.

- 6 T. butter, divided
- 1/4 c. all-purpose flour
- 2 c. milk
- 1 c. American cheese, shredded
- 1/4 c. slivered blanched almonds
- 3 to 4 potatoes, cooked and sliced
- 14-1/2 oz. can green beans, drained
- 2 c. smoked ham, cubed
- 1-1/2 c. soft bread crumbs

Melt 4 tablespoons butter in a saucepan over low heat; stir in flour. Gradually add milk, stirring constantly until thickened. Add cheese; heat slowly until melted. Stir in almonds; set aside. Arrange potato slices in a greased 2-quart casserole dish; top with green beans. Pour half of cheese mixture over green beans; top with ham and remaining cheese mixture. Melt remaining butter and toss with bread crumbs; sprinkle crumbs over casserole. Bake at 350 degrees for 30 to 35 minutes, or until crumbs are lightly golden. Serves 6 to 8.

An edible, glittery garnish...roll grapes, strawberries and blueberries in extra-fine sugar. Kids will eat 'em up!

Potatoes & Sausage Au Gratin

Tracy Walters
Denver, PA

With only 4 ingredients, the kids can whip up dinner!

16-oz. jar pasteurized processed cheese sauce, melted
16-oz. container sour cream
6 to 8 potatoes, peeled, cooked and diced
4 links smoked sausage, cut into bite-size pieces

Mix together melted cheese sauce and sour cream in a large bowl; stir in potatoes and sausage. Pour into an ungreased 13"x9" baking pan. Bake at 350 degrees for 35 minutes, until hot and bubbly.
Serves 6 to 8.

Sprinkle a flavorful seasoning onto casserole dishes before baking. Combine 1/4 cup coarse salt with 2 to 4 tablespoons mixed ground spices. Try combinations such as caraway seed and pepper, thyme and sesame seed or chili powder and dried oregano.

Pork Chops & Biscuit Stuffing

Barbara Girlardo
Pittsburgh, PA

Biscuits are the secret to this homestyle stuffing!

6 pork chops
1 T. oil
10-3/4 oz. can cream of
  chicken soup
1 c. celery, diced
1 c. onion, diced
1/4 t. pepper
1/8 t. poultry seasoning
1 egg
12-oz. tube refrigerated biscuits

Brown pork chops in oil in a large skillet over medium heat. Arrange chops in a greased 13"x9" baking pan; set aside. Combine remaining ingredients except biscuits in a mixing bowl; set aside. Using a pizza cutter, cut each biscuit into 8 pieces. Fold into soup mixture and spoon over chops. Bake at 350 degrees for 45 to 55 minutes, until biscuits are golden. Makes 6 servings.

What's the best way to keep mashed potatoes warm? Spoon potatoes into a heat-proof bowl over a pot filled with 3 inches of slightly simmering water. Cover with a lid or aluminum foil to trap the steam. Potatoes will stay warm for up to 2 hours!

Mile-High Pork Chop Casserole

Karen Shepherd
Elko, NV

Use red or yellow peppers for color and variety.

4 pork chops
salt and pepper to taste
2 T. oil
1 c. long-cooking rice, uncooked
1 tomato, sliced
1 green pepper, sliced
1 onion, sliced
10-oz. can beef consommé

Sprinkle pork chops on both sides with salt and pepper. Heat oil in a skillet; cook chops on both sides until golden. Set aside. Sprinkle rice in a lightly greased 11"x7" baking pan. Arrange pork chops on top of rice. Place tomato, green pepper and onion slices on top of each pork chop. Pour consommé over all; cover. Bake at 350 degrees for 1-1/2 hours, or until pork chops are tender and rice has absorbed all the liquid. Makes 4 servings.

When it's time to jazz up dinner with some new recipes, host a recipe swap party! Invite friends to bring a favorite casserole along with enough recipe cards for each guest. While everyone is enjoying the potluck of scrumptious food, collect the recipe cards, staple together and hand out before everyone goes home.

3-Bean & Ham Casserole

Melanie Lowe
Dover, DE

Hearty & filling...feeds a crowd!

10-oz. pkg. frozen lima beans, cooked
3 16-oz. cans baked beans, drained and rinsed
2 16-oz. cans kidney beans, drained and rinsed
1 lb. pork sausage links, sliced into 2-inch pieces
1/2 lb. smoked ham, cubed
1 T. salt
1-1/2 t. pepper
1/2 t. mustard
8-oz. can tomato sauce
1/2 c. catsup
1/4 c. brown sugar, packed
1 onion, chopped

Combine all ingredients in an ungreased 3-1/2 quart baking dish; mix well. Bake, uncovered, at 400 degrees for one hour. Makes 16 to 20 servings.

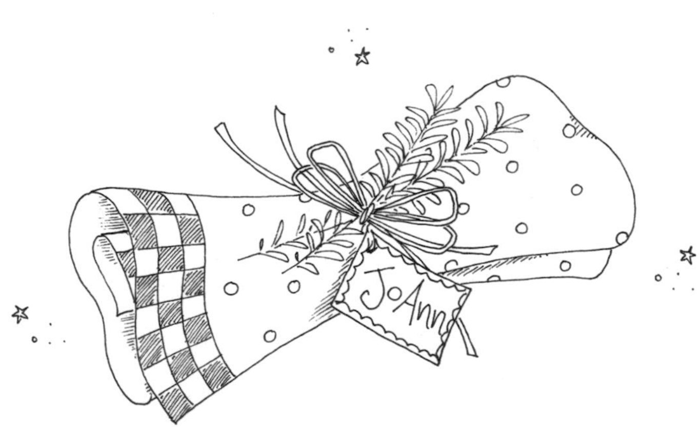

Make herbed butter in a jiffy...yummy on warm rolls or bread. Unwrap a stick of butter and cut in half lengthwise. Roll each half in freshly chopped herbs, then slice and serve.

Pork

Pork Chop Au Gratin

Linda Karner
Pisgah Forest, NC

I like to turn this recipe into Pork Chop Scallop by using a 7-ounce package of scalloped potato mix.

6 to 8 pork chops
1 t. salt
1 to 2 T. oil
2 c. water
2 carrots, peeled and thinly sliced
10-oz. pkg. frozen Italian green beans
2 T. butter
7-oz. pkg. au gratin potato mix
10-3/4 oz. can cream of celery soup
2/3 c. milk
2 T. Dijon mustard
1/2 t. dried basil
1/2 t. Worcestershire sauce

Sprinkle pork chops with salt. Brown in oil in a skillet over medium heat; set aside. Heat water to boiling in a saucepan; add carrots and beans. Return to a boil; stir in butter, potato slices and sauce from mix. Remove from heat and set aside. Mix soup, milk, mustard, basil and Worcestershire sauce; stir into vegetable mixture and pour into an ungreased 13"x9" baking pan. Arrange chops on top. Cover and bake at 350 degrees for 45 minutes; uncover and bake an additional 15 minutes, until chops are tender. Let stand 5 minutes before serving. Makes 6 to 8 servings.

For a clever twist, turn short-stemmed glasses upside-down and they become candle stands.

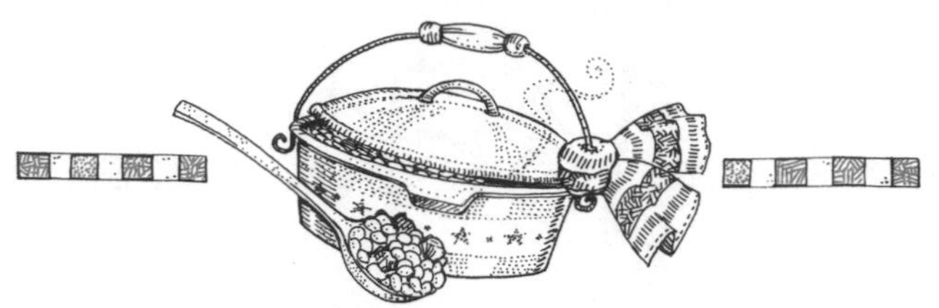

Mom's Green Bean Bake

Regina Vining
Warwick, RI

Adding sausage to a traditional favorite makes this recipe one of our family's favorite dinners.

2 10-3/4 oz. cans cream of mushroom soup
1 c. milk
1 T. soy sauce
1 clove garlic, minced
pepper to taste
1 lb. ground sausage, browned and drained
2 16-oz. pkgs. frozen cut green beans
2.8-oz. can French fried onions, divided

Combine soup, milk, soy sauce, garlic and pepper in a large bowl; mix well. Stir in sausage; add green beans and stir until evenly coated. Pour half the mixture into a greased 13"x9" baking pan; top with half the onions. Spread remaining sausage mixture over onions. Bake at 350 degrees for 30 minutes; sprinkle with remaining onions and bake an additional 5 to 10 minutes. Let stand 5 minutes before serving. Serves 8.

Kitchen magnets that are cute as a button! Look through Grandma's button box to find a variety of buttons. Hot-glue each button to a small magnet, and it's ready for the refrigerator door to keep recipes and shopping lists at your fingertips.

Hubby's Ham Casserole

Amy Butcher
Columbus, GA

My husband created this recipe and it's turned out to be a "must have" at our year 'round family get-togethers.

2 c. cooked ham, cubed
3 c. prepared elbow macaroni
10-3/4 oz. can cream of mushroom soup
3/4 c. shredded Cheddar cheese
3/4 c. milk
1/4 c. dry bread crumbs

Combine all ingredients except bread crumbs in an ungreased 13"x9" baking pan; mix well. Bake, covered, at 375 degrees for 20 minutes; remove cover and sprinkle with bread crumbs. Bake an additional 10 minutes. Serves 6.

Corral kitchen utensils with a playful candy wrapper pail. Apply découpage medium to the pail with a foam brush, smooth on wrappers, and then coat the wrappers with another coat of découpage medium.

Bermuda Pork & Rice

Anne DeGroff
Amsterdam, NY

This is one of those fond recipes that my mother used to prepare. I round out supper with peas and French bread rolls.

2 to 4 thick boneless pork chops
salt and pepper to taste
1/2 red onion, thinly sliced
1 c. long-cooking rice, uncooked
29-oz. can whole tomatoes, chopped
1 c. water

Sprinkle pork chops to taste with salt and pepper; place in a greased 13"x9" baking pan. Top with onion slices, rice and tomatoes with their juice. Pour water over top; cover with aluminum foil. Bake at 325 degrees for 3 hours. Serves 2 to 4.

To get a better grip on kitchen scissors, wrap their handles with soft linen and cotton twine.

Ham-It-Up Casserole

Lisa Bownas
Gooseberry Patch

Use thickly sliced steak fries and smoked ham to give this dish a brand-new flavor. Whatever you choose, you can't go wrong, it's always great tasting!

16-oz. pkg. frozen French fries
16-oz. pkg. frozen chopped broccoli, cooked
1-1/2 c. cooked ham, cubed
10-3/4 oz. can cream of mushroom soup
1-1/4 c. milk
1/4 c. mayonnaise
1 c. grated Parmesan cheese

Arrange fries in a greased 13"x9" baking pan. Top with broccoli; sprinkle with ham and set aside. Combine soup, milk and mayonnaise in a small bowl; mix well and pour evenly over ham. Sprinkle with cheese. Bake, uncovered, at 375 degrees for 40 minutes. Serves 4 to 6.

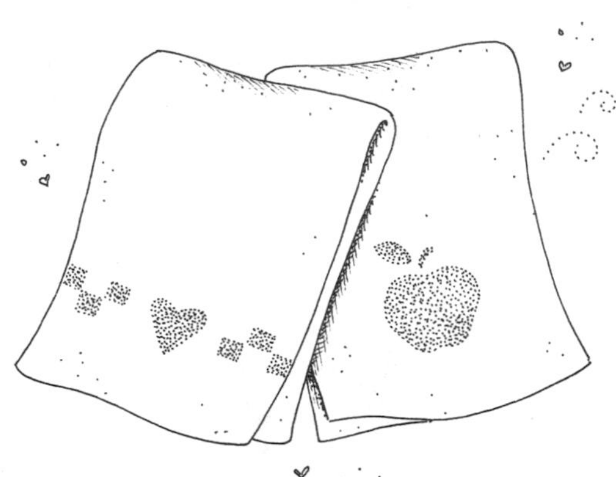

Stencil a set of kitchen tea towels and really perk up the kitchen. Lay a towel over a sheet of paper. Center the stencil on towel and, holding it firmly, apply 2 coats of washable fabric paint with a foam stencil brush. Remove stencil and let dry about 3 hours.

Best-Ever Cabbage & Rice

Nichole Martelli
Alvin, TX

My sister made this casserole many years ago and I loved it! Its cheesy topping makes this my favorite cabbage dish.

1 lb. ground sausage
1 lb. ground beef
2 to 3 stalks celery, chopped
1 onion, chopped
1/2 green pepper, chopped
1 clove garlic, minced
1 t. salt
1/4 t. pepper
1 head cabbage, chopped
10-oz. can tomatoes with chiles
1/4 c. water
1 c. long-cooking rice, uncooked
3 T. butter
1 T. all-purpose flour
1 c. pasteurized processed cheese spread, cubed
1 c. milk

Brown meats together in a large skillet over medium heat; drain. Add the next 6 ingredients to skillet and simmer for 5 minutes. Add cabbage, tomatoes with chiles, water and rice. Simmer for 5 additional minutes. Pour into an ungreased 13"x9" baking pan; set aside. Melt butter in a saucepan over low heat. Add flour and stir until smooth. Add cheese and milk; stir until cheese is melted. Pour sauce over cabbage mixture. Cover with aluminum foil and bake at 350 degrees for 1-1/2 hours. Serves 6 to 8.

Mix up homemade salad dressing…so fresh! Blend 1/2 cup mayonnaise, 3/4 cup olive oil, 1/3 cup red wine vinegar, 2 teaspoons salt and one teaspoon pepper. Drizzle over tossed salad or cooked pasta and veggies.

Use Your Noodle Casserole

Jason Keller
Carrollton, GA

Feeling creative in the kitchen, I pulled out all my tasty leftovers, tossed them together and invented this super casserole!

2 T. butter
2 T. all-purpose flour
1 c. milk
1/2 c. cooked ham, cubed
1/2 c. cooked chicken, cubed
1 c. prepared wide egg noodles
1/4 c. celery, chopped
1/4 t. salt
1/4 t. pepper
1/4 c. shredded Cheddar cheese
Optional: paprika to taste

Melt butter in a large saucepan over low heat; stir in flour and heat until bubbly. Slowly add milk, stirring constantly, until mixture is thick and smooth. Remove from heat; stir in ham, chicken, noodles, celery, salt and pepper. Transfer to an ungreased 1-1/2 quart casserole dish. Bake at 400 degrees for 15 minutes. Sprinkle with cheese and paprika, if using. Bake an additional 5 to 10 minutes, or until cheese is bubbly. Serves 4.

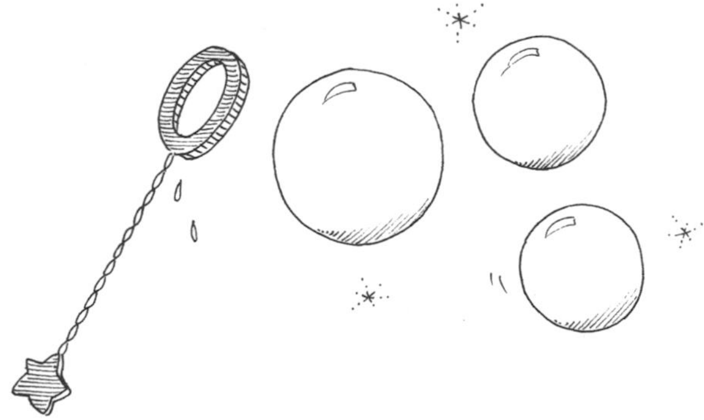

While dinner is in the oven, enjoy some time lazily blowing bubbles with the kids. The best bubble solution is a homemade recipe of 10 cups water plus 4 cups dish-washing liquid and one cup corn syrup.

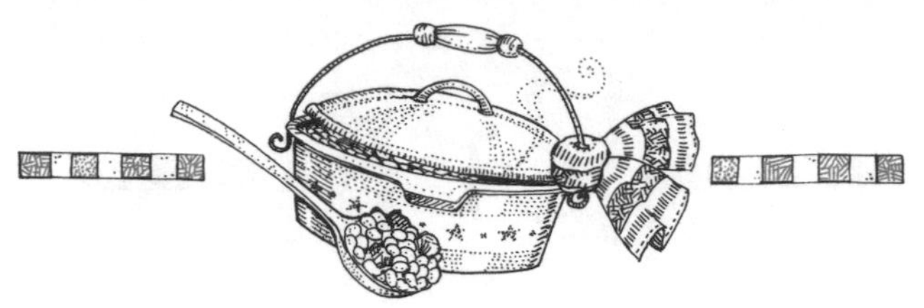

Oh-So-Easy Casserole

Kay Bradshaw
Rose Hill, NC

Ham and potatoes blended with Cheddar cheese...yum!

2 c. cooked ham, diced
32-oz. pkg. frozen hashbrowns, thawed
10-3/4 oz. can cream of mushroom soup
10-3/4 oz. can Cheddar cheese soup
salt and pepper to taste

Mix all ingredients together well; spoon into a lightly greased 9"x9" baking pan. Bake at 375 degrees for 45 to 60 minutes. Serves 4.

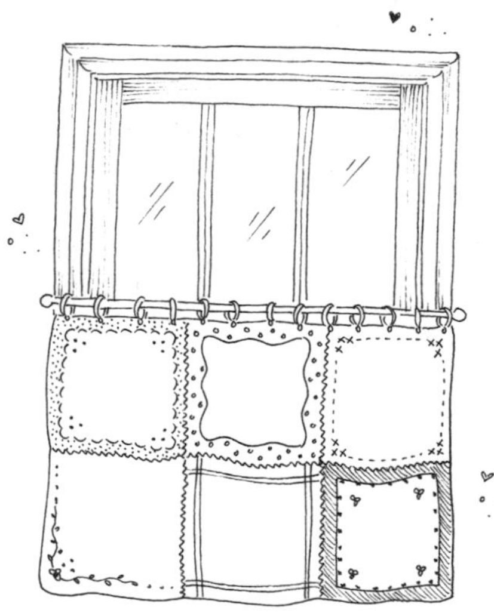

Add vintage flair to a kitchen window with flea-market find handkerchiefs. You can whip up a curtain in no time at all. Measure to see how many handkerchiefs are needed to cover the bottom half of a window, then join them together with a zig-zag stitch. Attach café hooks and hang from a rod...so easy.

Homestyle Pork Chops

Carole Foltman
Williams Bay, WI

When I'm short on time, I turn to this recipe. I can get it ready to pop in the oven in just a few minutes and yet it's elegant enough to serve company.

8 pork chops
1 T. margarine
1 green pepper, chopped
1 onion, chopped
10-3/4 oz. can cream of mushroom soup
16-oz. container sour cream

In a skillet over medium heat, brown chops in margarine. Arrange chops in an ungreased 13"x9" baking pan. Mix remaining ingredients and pour over chops. Bake at 300 degrees for one hour. Makes 8 servings.

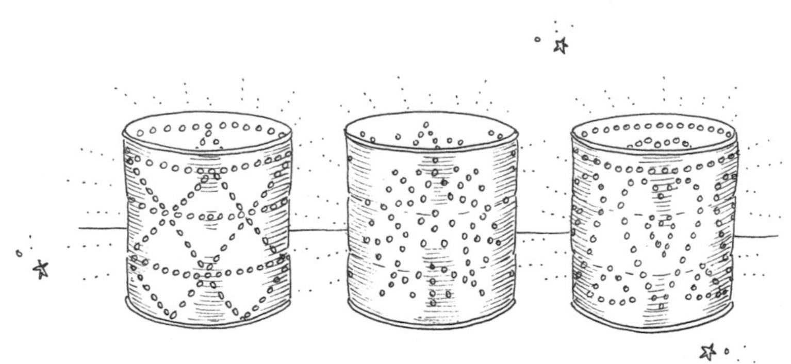

Put those clean, empty coffee cans to use as porch lanterns. Remove the labels and fill each can with water and freeze. Steady a frozen can on a bag of rice, then create a design by punching holes with an awl and hammer. Defrost and dry cans and paint exterior with oil-based enamel.

Country Ham & Potato Pie

Jennifer Switala
Selinsgrove, PA

I usually set a baking sheet under the pie while it bakes to catch any spills from bubbling over.

2 potatoes, peeled and sliced
2 c. cooked ham, cubed
1 onion, sliced
2 c. shredded Cheddar cheese
3 T. all-purpose flour
1 t. garlic salt
1/4 t. pepper
1/8 t. nutmeg
1 c. milk
1 T. margarine, diced
9-inch pie crust
1/2 c. whipping cream

Layer potatoes, ham and onion in a lightly greased 9" round baking pan; set aside. Mix together cheese, flour, garlic salt, pepper and nutmeg; sprinkle over ham mixture. Pour milk over the top; dot with margarine. Place pie crust on top; cut 4 slits in the center. Bake at 350 degrees for one hour; remove from oven. Pour cream into slits of crust; let stand for 10 minutes. Cut into wedges to serve.
Makes 4 to 6 servings.

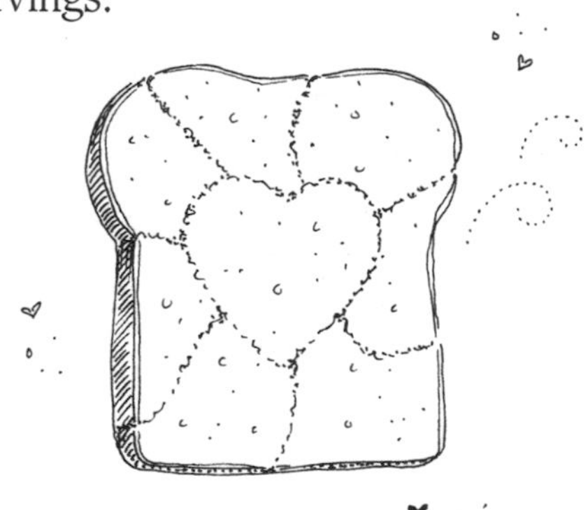

Turn bread slices into puzzles...dinnertime fun for the kids! Butter bread slices and use a cookie cutter to slice a shape through the center. Then cut the surrounding puzzle pieces with a kitchen knife in any shape. Scramble the pieces before serving the sandwich.

Parmesan Potatoes & Ham

Stephanie Mayer
Portsmouth, VA

Creamy soups are so versatile...this recipe uses celery, but try mushroom, chicken or potato too.

10-3/4 oz. can cream of celery soup
1/2 c. milk
pepper to taste
2 potatoes, peeled and sliced
1 onion, sliced
2 c. cooked ham, diced
2 T. grated Parmesan cheese

Combine soup, milk and pepper in an ungreased 8"x8" baking pan. Layer potatoes, onion and ham over top. Bake, covered, at 375 degrees for one hour. Sprinkle with cheese and bake, uncovered for an additional 20 minutes. Serves 6.

Make everyday dishes anything but ordinary. Porcelain paint, available at crafts stores, comes in tubes with pen-like tips. Even the kids can create a one-of-a-kind dish just for them! Allow the paint to dry, and then set the paint by baking the dishes in the oven according to the directions on the tube's label.

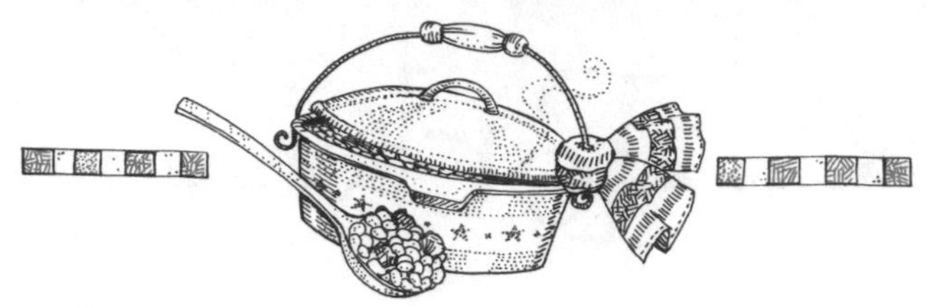

Crunchy Almond & Sausage Bake

Athena Colegrove
Big Springs, TX

A yummy mix of ingredients I grew up loving. Now I make it for my family & friends.

1 lb. sausage link, sliced
1/4 c. onion, sliced
1 stalk celery, chopped
1 green pepper, chopped
1/2 c. long-grain rice, uncooked
4-1/2 oz. pkg. chicken noodle soup mix
2 c. hot water
1/2 c. slivered almonds

Combine sausage, onion, celery and green pepper in a large skillet over medium-high heat. Sauté for 5 minutes; drain. Stir in rice, soup mix and water. Transfer to a lightly greased 2-quart casserole dish; sprinkle with almonds. Bake, covered, at 300 degrees for 1-1/2 hours. Serves 6.

Fruit butter is yummy spread on dinner rolls. Combine 1/2 cup softened butter with one cup powdered sugar and one to 2 cups sliced berries or fruit. Place in a food processor and process until smooth. Refrigerate and use within one week.

Savory Pork Tenderloin

Vickie

Tender pork over sage dressing...oh, my!

3 potatoes, thinly sliced
1-1/4 c. milk, divided
salt and pepper to taste
1-1/2 c. bread crumbs
1/2 t. salt
1/4 t. dried sage
2 T. plus 2 t. butter, diced and divided
2 T. onion, minced
1 lb. pork tenderloin, sliced 1/2-inch thick

Place potatoes in a well greased 2-quart casserole dish. Add one cup milk; sprinkle with salt and pepper. Combine remaining milk, bread crumbs, salt, sage, 2 teaspoons butter and minced onion. Spread over potatoes; set aside. Flatten pork slices with a mallet until 1/4-inch thick. Arrange over bread crumbs and dot with remaining butter. Bake, covered, at 350 degrees for 1-1/2 hours. Serves 4 to 6.

Laughter is brightest where food is best.
-Irish Proverb

Speedy Ham & Beans

Julie Sibbersen
Portage, MI

Ready in 20 minutes!

1-1/3 c. prepared instant rice
14-oz. can green beans, drained
5-oz. can chopped ham
1/3 c. mayonnaise
1 t. chicken bouillon granules
1-1/3 c. boiling water
1 T. dried, minced onion
1/2 c. shredded Cheddar cheese

Combine rice, green beans, ham and mayonnaise in a lightly greased 11"x7" baking pan; set aside. Dissolve bouillon in water; pour over rice mixture. Sprinkle with minced onion and mix well. Bake at 400 degrees for 15 minutes; sprinkle with cheese and bake an additional 5 minutes, or until cheese is melted. Makes 4 to 6 servings.

Bring a bit of summer vacation to the kitchen sink…a clam or scallop shell is the perfect size for holding a bar of soap!

Vegetable

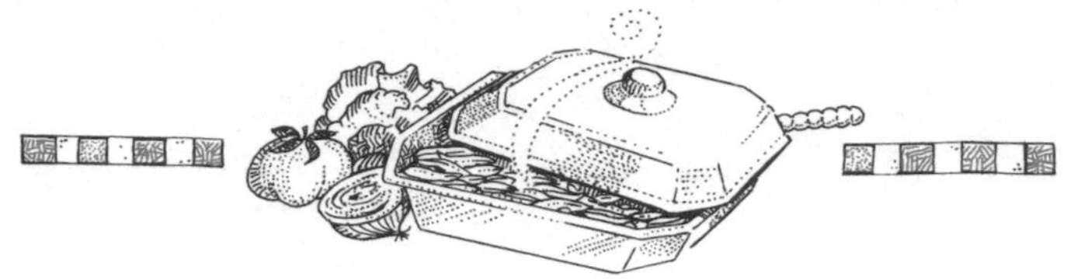

Easy Chiles Rellenos

Celeste Fong
Upland, CA

A quick-to-fix dish that's sure to become a tradition in your home.

1/2 c. butter
7-oz. can chopped green chiles
2 16-oz. pkgs. shredded
Mexican-blend cheese
1 c. biscuit baking mix
3/4 t. salt
3 eggs
2 c. milk

Melt butter in a 13"x9" baking pan. Sprinkle chiles over butter; top with cheese and set aside. Blend baking mix, salt, eggs and milk in a blender; pour over cheese. Bake at 350 degrees for 35 to 40 minutes. Serves 12.

Salt & pepper shakers make the best bud vases! They're just the right size and come in so many whimsical styles.

Garden-Fresh Tortilla Bake

Dianna Likens
Gooseberry Patch

Great with homemade salsa and lots of crispy chips alongside.

2 T. oil
1 lb. zucchini, sliced
1 onion, chopped
1 green pepper, chopped
7-oz. can diced green chiles
4 eggs, hard-boiled, peeled and chopped
salt, pepper and ground cumin to taste
2 T. all-purpose flour
1 c. sour cream
6 6-inch corn tortillas, cut into 6 wedges
3 c. shredded Cheddar cheese

Heat oil in a skillet over medium heat; add zucchini, onion and green pepper. Cook until vegetables are just tender, about 5 minutes. Remove from heat; stir in chiles, eggs, salt, pepper and cumin; set aside. Blend flour into sour cream until smooth; set aside. Arrange tortilla wedges in an ungreased 2-quart casserole dish. Layer with half the vegetable mixture, half the sour cream mixture and half the cheese. Repeat layers. Bake, uncovered, at 350 degrees for 30 minutes or until bubbly. Serves 6.

Whip up this simple salad dressing to serve on a crispy bed of lettuce alongside Garden-Fresh Tortilla Bake. Blend 1/2 cup catsup, 1 cup oil, 3/4 cup sugar, 1/4 cup vinegar and 1 tablespoon hot pepper sauce...olé!

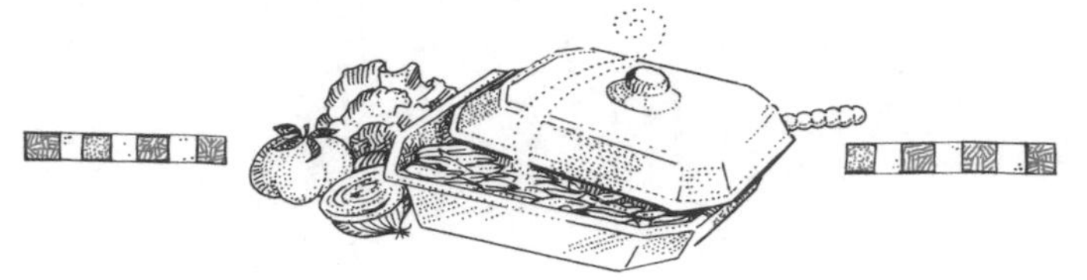

Summertime Squash Casserole

Melissa Currie
Phoenix, AZ

I love to make this when there is a bounty of squash in my garden!

1 c. shredded Cheddar cheese
1/2 c. cottage cheese
4 eggs, beaten
3 T. butter, melted
3/4 c. bread crumbs
1 T. parsley, chopped
1 T. salt
1/2 t. pepper
2 lbs. yellow squash, sliced

Mix all ingredients together, adding the squash last. Pour into an ungreased 13"x9" baking pan. Bake at 350 degrees for 45 minutes. Serves 6 to 8.

Fill tiny terra cotta pots with votive candles, then march them right down the center of a buffet table...so pretty. In summer, use citronella votives for outdoor picnic tables.

Herbed Veggie-Cheese Casserole

Jo Ann

Three veggies combine for a delectable cheesy dish.

10-oz. pkg. frozen green beans
10-oz. pkg. frozen broccoli
10-oz. pkg. frozen cauliflower
10-oz. jar pearl onions, drained
1 c. shredded Cheddar cheese
2 10-3/4 oz. cans cream of mushroom soup
6-oz. pkg. herb stuffing mix

Cook frozen vegetables separately, just until crisp-tender. Arrange drained vegetables in layers in a greased 13"x9" baking pan. Arrange onions around the outer edge. Sprinkle with cheese; pour soup over all. Bake at 350 degrees for 30 minutes. Remove from oven; sprinkle half the stuffing over the top, reserving the rest for another recipe. Bake for an additional 15 minutes. Serves 8.

When family & friends are staying for the weekend, make the guest room extra special. Fill a vase with blooming flowers, set out a few favorite books or magazines and give the sheets a spritz with lavender spray.

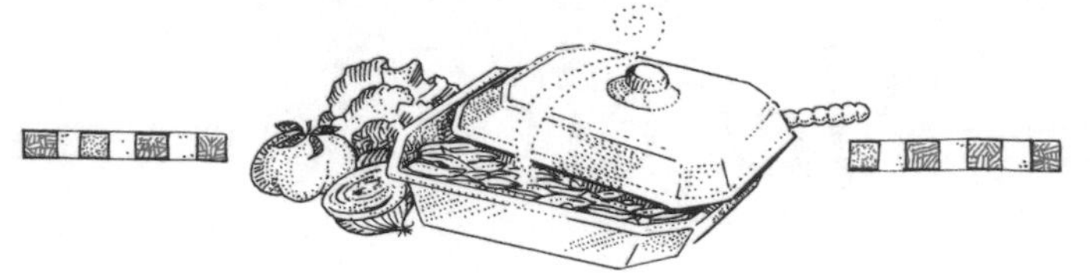

Fast & Fresh Asparagus Casserole

Kelly Alderson
Erie, PA

The crunch of water chestnuts sets this casserole apart.

1 lb. carrots, peeled, sliced and cooked
15-oz. can asparagus spears, drained
15-1/4 oz. can peas, drained
8-oz. can sliced water chestnuts, drained
3 eggs, hard-boiled, peeled and sliced
1/3 c. butter
10-3/4 oz. can cream of mushroom soup
1 c. shredded Cheddar cheese, divided
1 c. cracker crumbs
1/2 t. pepper

Layer carrots, asparagus and peas in a lightly greased 13"x9" baking pan. Place water chestnuts and sliced eggs over vegetables. Dot with butter. Mix soup and 3/4 cup cheese; spread over vegetable layers. Bake at 350 degrees for 30 minutes or until bubbly. Sprinkle with crumbs, pepper and remaining cheese; bake an additional 5 minutes or until cheese melts. Serves 6 to 8.

Freezing cheese causes it to turn crumbly, and while that isn't good for a recipe using fresh cheese, it's ideal in baked casserole dishes! Just thaw cheese in the refrigerator and use within a few days.

Old-Fashioned Potato Casserole

Delynn Flinn
Bradenton, FL

Simple ingredients for a homestyle taste your family will love.

28-oz. pkg. frozen hashbrowns with onions and peppers
2 10-3/4 oz. cans cream of chicken soup
16-oz. container sour cream
2 c. shredded Cheddar cheese
2 c. corn flake cereal, crushed
1/2 c. butter, melted

Spread hashbrowns in a lightly greased 13"x9" baking pan. Mix soup and sour cream together; spread on top of hashbrowns. Sprinkle with cheese; top with crushed corn flakes. Drizzle butter over all. Bake at 350 degrees for 30 to 35 minutes. Serves 6 to 8.

Decorate for reunions and gatherings with flea-market finds...so clever! A weathered watering can filled with black-eyed Susans becomes a centerpiece, while vintage metal picnic tins can hold everything from napkins and silverware to wax paper-wrapped sandwiches.

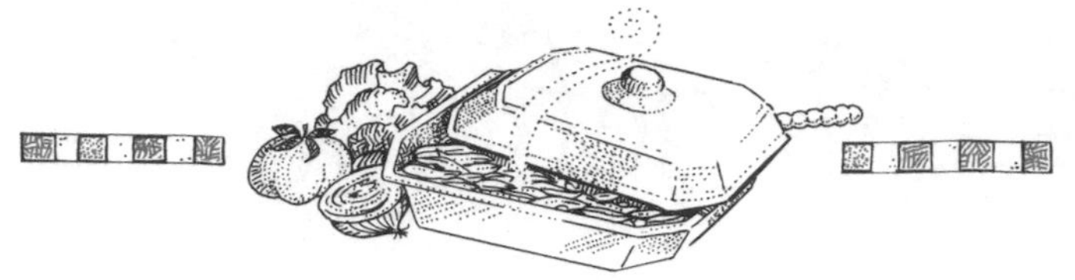

Eggplant Parmesan

Tammy Dillow
Raceland, KY

For me, this is a down-home dish that's great to enjoy with family & friends no matter what the occasion.

4 eggs, beaten
3 T. water
2 medium eggplants, peeled and sliced 1/4-inch thick
2 c. Italian-style bread crumbs
1-1/2 c. grated Parmesan cheese, divided
27-3/4 oz. jar garden-style pasta sauce, divided
1-1/2 c. shredded mozzarella cheese

Combine eggs and water in a shallow bowl. Dip eggplant slices into egg mixture. Arrange slices in a single layer on a greased baking sheet; bake at 350 degrees for 25 minutes or until golden. Set aside. Mix bread crumbs and 1/2 cup Parmesan cheese; set aside. Spread a small amount of sauce in an ungreased 13"x9" baking pan; layer half the eggplant, one cup sauce and one cup crumb mixture. Repeat layering. Cover with aluminum foil and bake for 45 minutes. Remove cover; sprinkle with mozzarella cheese. Bake, uncovered, for an additional 10 minutes. Cut into squares. Serves 6 to 8.

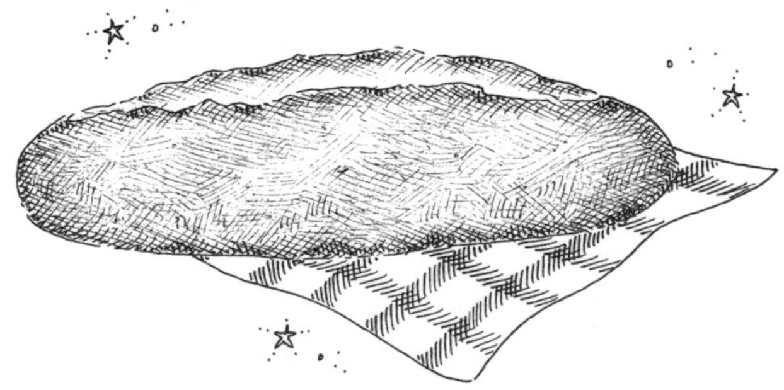

Fresh bread crumbs are a snap! Just place Italian bread cubes in a food processor and pulse until the texture becomes fine.

Creamy Asparagus Casserole

Angela Murphy
Tempe, AZ

A sure-fire family favorite!

15-oz. can asparagus spears, drained
10-3/4 oz. can cream of mushroom soup
1-1/2 c. prepared rice
1 onion, finely chopped
1 c. shredded Cheddar cheese

Combine all ingredients and places in a greased 11"x7" baking pan. Cover and bake at 325 degrees for 30 minutes. Serves 4 to 6.

It's true...place an onion in the freezer for just 5 minutes before chopping for no tears!

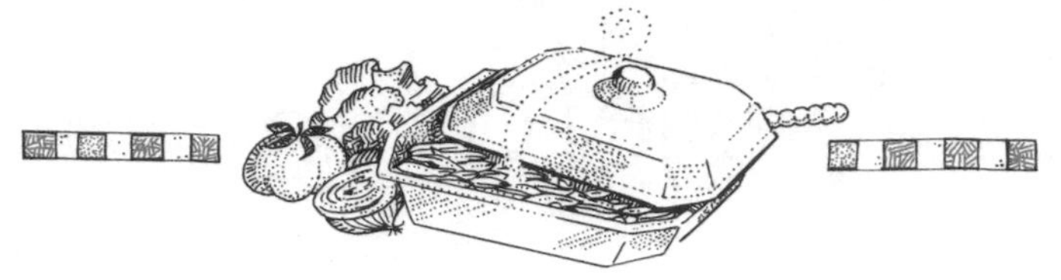

Gardeners' Casserole

Kathy Fortune
Wooster, OH

A winning combination of fresh-from-the-garden flavors!

1 head cauliflower, chopped
1 head broccoli, chopped
8 carrots, peeled and sliced 1-inch thick
1 t. fresh chives, minced
salt and pepper to taste
1 onion, chopped
1/2 c. butter
1/4 c. all-purpose flour
8-oz. container whipping cream
2 c. milk
8-oz. pkg. cream cheese, softened
1 c. shredded Cheddar cheese
1 c. seasoned croutons, crushed

Steam cauliflower, broccoli and carrots until crisp-tender. Place vegetables in a lightly greased 13"x9" baking pan; sprinkle with chives, salt and pepper. Set aside. In a saucepan over medium heat, sauté onion in butter; gradually add flour, stirring constantly. Stir in cream and milk; add cream cheese, stirring constantly until thick and smooth. Pour cheese sauce over vegetables and mix gently. Sprinkle with cheese and croutons. Bake at 325 degrees for 30 to 35 minutes. Serves 8.

Did you know you can freeze casseroles baked or unbaked? It's best to let the surface of the casserole freeze, then wrap the entire baking pan tightly with plastic wrap or aluminum foil. Don't forget to add extra time to the original baking directions.

Oniony Zucchini Bake

Pam Messner
Gibbon, MN

When the zucchini is bursting in my garden, this is the recipe I turn to. It just can't be beat for taste.

3 c. zucchini, thinly sliced
4 eggs, beaten
1 c. biscuit baking mix
1/2 c. oil
1/2 c. onion, chopped
1/2 c. grated Parmesan cheese
2 T. fresh parsley, chopped
1/2 t. seasoned salt
1/2 t. dried oregano
1/2 t. salt
1/4 t. pepper

Mix all ingredients together. Pour into a greased 13"x9" baking pan. Bake at 350 degrees for 30 minutes. Serves 6 to 8.

What can you serve with casseroles? Crisp salads, grilled vegetables, buttered new potatoes or fresh fruit salads are all perfect pairings!

Potatoes Romanoff

Sally Borland
Port Gibson, NY

Feeds a crowd...just right for picnics and potlucks.

6 to 9 c. potatoes, peeled, cooked and cubed
salt to taste
2 c. cottage cheese
1 c. sour cream
1/4 c. onion, minced
garlic powder to taste
1/2 c. shredded Cheddar cheese

Sprinkle potatoes with salt. Combine with cottage cheese, sour cream, onion and garlic powder. Pour into an ungreased 1-1/2 quart casserole dish. Top with cheese. Bake at 350 degrees for 40 to 50 minutes. Makes 12 to 14 servings.

Practical and easy to use, kitchen shears are so handy. You'll find yourself using them again & again for snipping fresh herbs, cutting canned tomatoes right in the can and cutting the ends off fresh green beans. Just remember to wash them with soap and water after each use.

Creamed Corn Casserole

Susan Hopewell
Northumberland, PA

A simple recipe that's big on taste.

1/2 c. butter, melted and divided
1 onion, chopped
1 green pepper, chopped
1 red pepper, chopped
3 eggs
1 c. sour cream
15-1/4 oz. can creamed corn
1/3 c. yellow cornmeal
1/4 t. salt
1/4 t. pepper
1 c. shredded Cheddar cheese

Combine 2 tablespoons butter, onion and peppers in a pan; cook over medium heat until softened. Remove from heat. In a separate bowl, combine remaining butter, eggs and sour cream; whisk together until smooth. Mix in corn, cornmeal, salt and pepper; stir in cheese and onion mixture. Place in a greased 13"x9" baking pan. Bake at 350 degrees for 40 to 45 minutes, until firm. Serves 6 to 8.

May happiness of heart & home be one, and may all who enter be enveloped in its warmth.

-Unknown

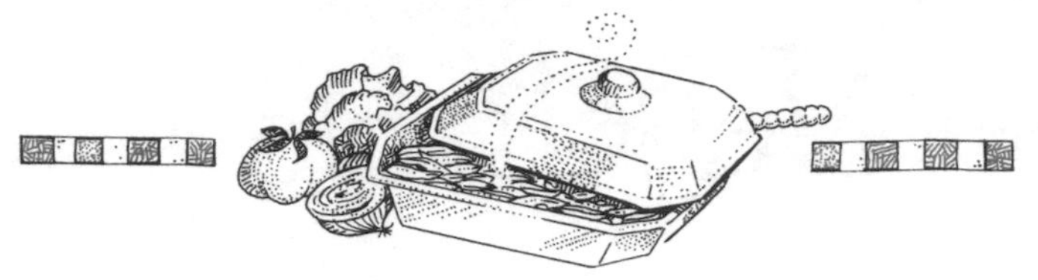

Mary's Broccoli & Rice

Mary Dishman
Evansville, IN

Sprinkle with shredded Cheddar to make it extra cheesy.

1/2 onion, chopped
1/2 c. plus 1 T. butter, melted and divided
15-oz. jar pasteurized processed cheese sauce
10-oz. pkg. frozen broccoli, thawed
10-3/4 oz. can cream of celery soup
1-1/2 c. instant rice, uncooked
1/2 c. milk
1/2 c. cracker crumbs

Sauté onion in 1/2 cup butter. Add cheese sauce, broccoli, soup, rice and milk; place in a greased 11"x7" baking pan. Set aside. Combine cracker crumbs and remaining butter; stir to coat and sprinkle over casserole. Bake at 350 degrees for 50 minutes to one hour. Serves 4 to 6.

Serve up homemade lemonade for a refreshing change…it couldn't be simpler! In a large saucepan, combine 2 quarts water and 1/2 cup sugar. Heat just until the sugar dissolves. Remove from heat and pour in 3/4 cup lemon juice. Mix well and chill.

Pierogie Casserole

Cheryl Lagler
Zionsville, PA

Bow tie pasta is also perfect in this recipe if you have them handy in the pantry.

- 4 onions, chopped
- 6 T. butter, divided
- 6 c. potatoes, peeled and boiled
- 1/2 c. chicken broth
- 1/2 to 1 c. milk
- salt and pepper to taste
- 2 eggs, beaten
- 1/4 c. shredded Cooper or Colby cheese
- 1/4 to 1/2 c. shredded Cheddar cheese
- 16-oz. pkg. mafalda pasta, cooked

Sauté onions in 2 tablespoons butter; set aside. Mash potatoes with broth, milk, remaining butter, salt and pepper. Add eggs and cheeses; mix well. Layer pasta, potatoes and onions in a greased 13"x9" baking pan. Bake at 350 degrees for 30 minutes. Serves 12.

Choose russet potatoes for casserole dishes...they're the best potato for baking. You'll need about 3 medium russets to equal one pound or approximately 3-1/2 cups chopped potatoes.

Golden Macaroni & Cheese

Carol Alexander
Colleyville, TX

A baked version that's a hit with kids and adults.

1 onion, chopped
1 clove garlic, chopped
1 T. butter
10-3/4 oz. can tomato soup
3/4 c. water
1/2 c. milk
16-oz. pkg. pasteurized processed cheese spread, cubed
8-oz. pkg. elbow macaroni, cooked

Sauté onion and garlic in butter until transparent; add soup, water, milk and cheese. Cook over medium heat, stirring occasionally, until well blended; add macaroni. Spoon into a 13"x9" baking pan; bake at 325 degrees for 45 minutes. Serves 6 to 8.

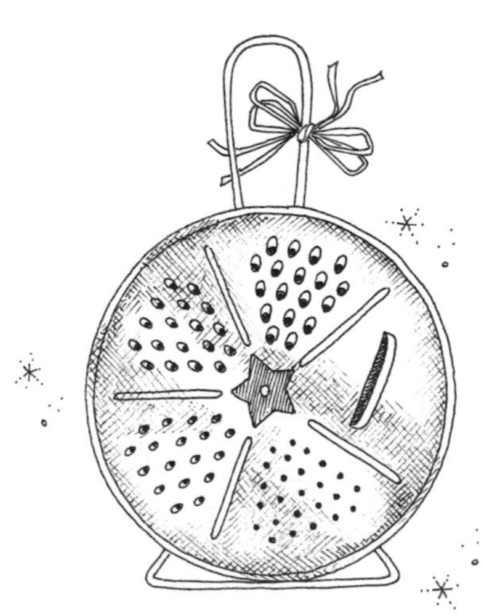

Try a new topping on casserole dishes...sprinkle on shredded cheese, fresh bread crumbs or crushed chow mein noodles. And to keep the topping crisp, don't cover the casserole dish during baking.

Ziti with Spinach & Cheese

Karen Pilcher
Burleson, TX

Wow...this recipe has 3 types of cheese!

2 10-oz. pkgs. frozen chopped spinach, cooked and drained
15-oz. container ricotta cheese
3 eggs, beaten
2/3 c. grated Parmesan cheese
1/4 t. pepper
16-oz. pkg. ziti pasta, cooked
28-oz. jar spaghetti sauce
2 t. dried oregano
12-oz. pkg. shredded mozzarella cheese

Combine spinach, ricotta cheese, eggs, Parmesan cheese and pepper; set aside. Combine pasta, spaghetti sauce and oregano; place half the pasta mixture in an ungreased 13"x9" baking pan. Layer with spinach mixture and mozzarella. Add remaining pasta mixture. Cover with aluminum foil and bake at 375 degrees for 25 minutes. Uncover and bake another 5 minutes, or until bubbly. Remove from the oven and let stand for about 10 minutes before serving. Serves 8.

To give your warm-from-the-oven bread loaf a slightly sweet glaze, just brush it with honey. Yum!

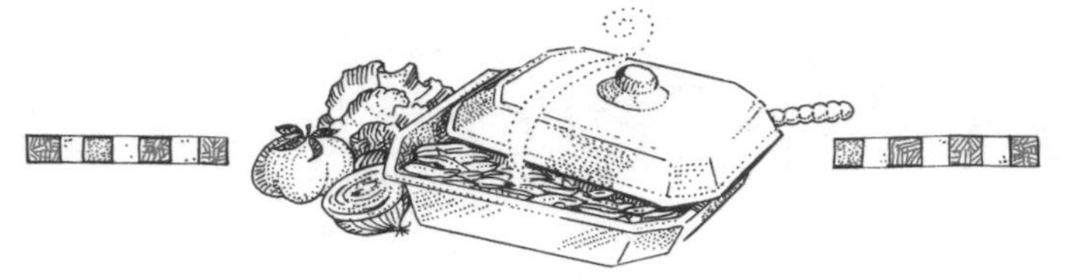

Ranchero Macaroni Bake

Sharon Crider
Lebanon, MO

Sprinkle with crushed blue tortilla chips instead...just because!

26-oz. can cream of mushroom soup
1 c. milk
6 c. prepared elbow macaroni
3 c. shredded Cheddar cheese
1 c. salsa
1 c. tortilla chips, coarsely crushed

In a large bowl, combine soup and milk. Stir in macaroni, cheese and salsa. Spoon into an ungreased 3-quart casserole dish. Bake at 400 degrees for 20 minutes. Stir; sprinkle with tortilla chips. Bake an additional 5 minutes, or until bubbly. Serves 8.

Turn any casserole into an overnight time-saver. Simply prepare a favorite casserole recipe the night before, cover and refrigerate. Just add 15 to 20 extra minutes to the baking time!

Tangy Corn Casserole

Dave Slyh
Galloway, OH

Great for brunch and summertime celebrations.

10-oz. pkg. frozen corn, thawed and drained
1/2 c. onion, chopped
1/2 c. green pepper, sliced into strips
1/2 c. water
1 c. yellow squash, chopped
1 tomato, chopped
1 c. shredded Cheddar cheese, divided
2/3 c. cornmeal
1/2 c. milk
2 eggs, beaten
3/4 t. salt
1/4 t. pepper
1/4 t. hot pepper sauce
Garnish: tomato slices, green pepper, sliced into rings

In a medium saucepan, combine corn, onion, green pepper and water. Bring to a boil; reduce to medium-low heat. Cover and simmer for 5 minutes, or until vegetables are crisp-tender. Do not drain. In a large mixing bowl, combine squash, tomato, 3/4 cup cheese, cornmeal, milk, eggs, salt, pepper and hot pepper sauce. Add corn mixture to cornmeal mixture; stir to blend. Turn into a greased 1-1/2 quart casserole dish. Bake at 350 degrees for 45 to 50 minutes, or until heated through. Top with remaining cheese, tomato slices and green pepper rings. Serves 8.

To keep eggs their freshest, be sure to store them in the carton...it prevents them from absorbing aromas from other foods in the refrigerator.

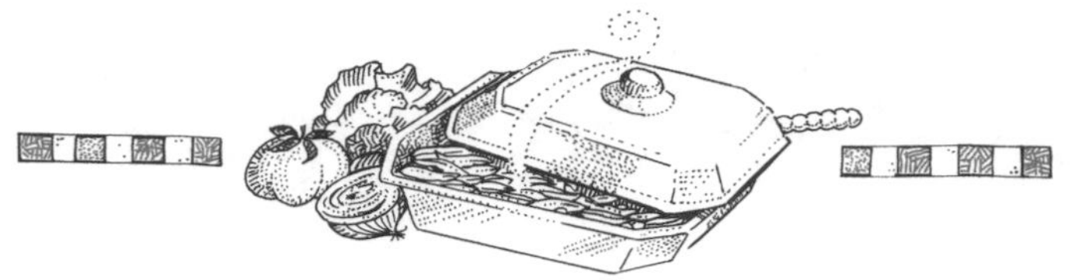

Very Veggie Lasagna

Tina Nanney
Chandler, AZ

Better than any restaurant lasagna...and I've tried many.

3 zucchini, sliced
8-oz. can mushrooms, drained and chopped
1 onion, chopped
4 cloves garlic, minced
3 T. olive oil
2 15-oz. containers ricotta cheese
1/4 c. grated Parmesan cheese
2 eggs
1 T. Italian seasoning
1/4 t. garlic salt
1/4 t. pepper
28-oz. jar spaghetti sauce, divided
16-oz. pkg. lasagna, cooked
28-oz. can crushed tomatoes, divided
16-oz. pkg. shredded mozzarella cheese, divided
2 T. dried parsley

Sauté first 4 ingredients in olive oil for 5 minutes; set aside. In a medium bowl, combine ricotta cheese, Parmesan cheese, eggs and seasonings. In an ungreased 13"x9" baking pan, place one cup spaghetti sauce, then a layer of lasagna strips. Spread half the sautéed vegetables on top of lasagna. Top with half the ricotta mixture. Top with next layer of lasagna and one cup tomatoes. Place remaining vegetables and ricotta mixture on top; sprinkle with one cup mozzarella cheese. Arrange remaining lasagna strips and spread remaining sauce and tomatoes over lasagna. Sprinkle with remaining mozzarella cheese and top with parsley. Cover with aluminum foil and bake at 375 degrees for one hour. Uncover; bake an additional 5 minutes. Turn off oven and leave in for 20 minutes. Serves 12.

Did you know that if you add 1/2 teaspoon uncooked rice to a salt shaker, it keeps the salt from clogging in the shaker?

20-Minute Veggie Bake

Janice Lewis
Mansfield, OH

Tasty hot or cold...just slice some garlic bread and dinner is served.

8-oz. pkg. elbow macaroni, cooked
1 onion, chopped
1/2 c. celery, chopped
1 green pepper, chopped
8-oz. can sliced mushrooms, drained
1/4 c. oil
garlic salt to taste
1 t. salt
1/4 t. pepper
1/2 c. green olives with pimentos, chopped
6-oz. can tomato paste
1 c. water
1/2 c. grated Parmesan cheese

Place macaroni in a lightly greased 2-quart casserole dish; set aside. In a skillet, sauté onion, celery, green pepper and mushrooms in oil until tender. Add seasonings, olives, tomato paste and water; simmer for 10 minutes. Pour over macaroni; top with cheese. Bake at 375 degrees for 20 minutes. Serves 4 to 6.

Keep veggies fresh longer by wrapping them in paper towels and storing in open plastic zipping bags in the refrigerator.

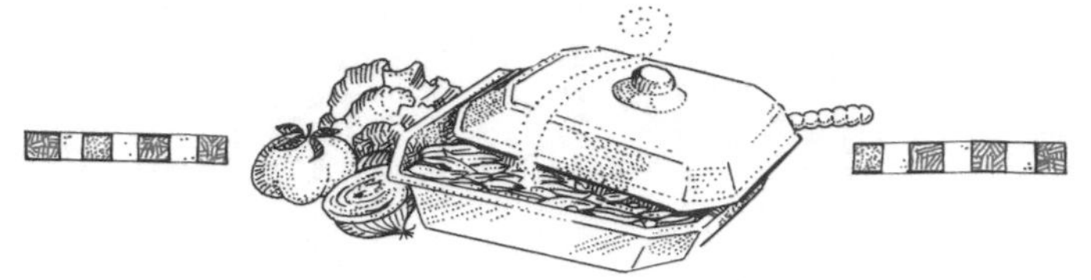

Spinach & Black Bean Lasagna

Michele Bartolomea
Stafford, VA

The secret is the fresh cilantro.

- 2 eggs, beaten
- 16-oz. container ricotta cheese
- 10-oz. frozen spinach, thawed and drained
- 1/2 t. salt
- 1/4 c. fresh cilantro, chopped
- 2 c. shredded Monterey Jack cheese
- 2 c. shredded Pepper Jack cheese
- 2 16-oz. cans black beans, drained and rinsed
- 2 13-oz. jars spaghetti sauce
- 1/2 t. ground cumin
- 12 strips no-boil lasagna

Mix eggs, ricotta cheese, spinach, salt and cilantro in a medium bowl; set aside. In a second bowl, combine Monterey Jack and Pepper Jack cheeses. Set aside. Mash beans with sauce and cumin in a third bowl; mix well. In a lightly greased 13"x9" baking pan, layer lasagna alternately with spinach mixture, cheese mixture and bean mixture, ending with remaining lasagna. Cover with aluminum foil and bake at 350 degrees for 45 minutes. Serves 9 to 12.

Are there extra biscuits after dinner? For a yummy dessert, split and top each half with sliced strawberries and a dollop of whipped cream.

Easy Cheesy Bowtie Pasta

Elissa Ducar
Denton, TX

A filling meal all by itself!

1/4 c. butter
1/4 c. all-purpose flour
1-1/2 c. milk
28-oz. can whole Italian tomatoes, drained, chopped and 1-1/4 c. liquid reserved
salt and pepper to taste
16-oz. pkg. bowtie pasta, cooked
1-1/2 c. grated mozzarella cheese
1/2 c. crumbled Gorgonzola cheese
1/2 c. shredded fontina cheese
1-1/3 c. grated Romano cheese, divided
1/2 c. fresh parsley, finely chopped

Melt butter over medium heat in a heavy saucepan. Add flour and whisk for 3 minutes. Add milk and reserved tomato juice gradually, whisking constantly. Bring to a boil. Stir in tomatoes, salt and pepper. Reduce heat to medium-low; let simmer for about 3 minutes, or until thickened. Set aside. Combine pasta, mozzarella, Gorgonzola, fontina, one cup Romano and parsley in a large bowl; stir in tomato mixture. Pour into a greased 4-quart casserole dish; sprinkle with remaining Romano cheese. Bake at 375 degrees for 30 to 35 minutes, or until bubbly. Let stand for 10 minutes before serving. Serves 6.

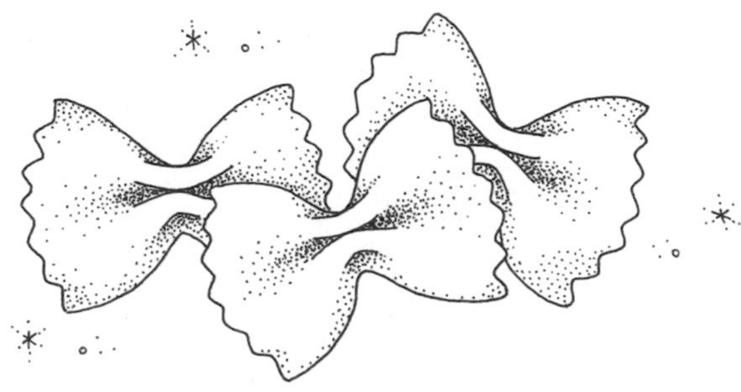

When cooking pasta, remember that rubbing a bit of vegetable oil around the top of the pot will prevent boilovers!

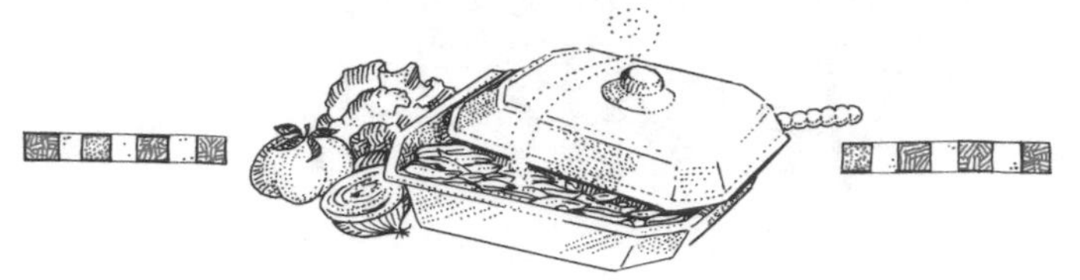

Mom's Broccoli Casserole

Joan Melo
Doylestown, PA

Mom was such a good cook, she could take nothing and turn it into something delicious! She was a truly wonderful lady.

2 c. cauliflowerets
1 c. carrots, peeled and sliced
24-oz. pkg. frozen broccoli, thawed and drained
1/2 c. margarine, melted
10-3/4 oz. can cream of mushroom soup
1 c. mayonnaise
1 c. shredded sharp Cheddar cheese
1/2 c. onion, chopped
1 c. buttery round crackers, crushed

Bring a large pot of water to a rapid boil; add cauliflower, carrots and broccoli. Boil only until vegetables are crisp-tender. Drain and set aside. Pour margarine into a 2-quart casserole dish; add vegetables and set aside. In a separate bowl, mix together soup, mayonnaise, cheese and onion. Spread mixture over vegetables. Top with crushed crackers. Bake at 350 degrees for 30 to 40 minutes. Serves 8.

Cauliflower is nothing but cabbage with a college education.
-Mark Twain

Farmers' Market Casserole

Brad Warner
Worthington, OH

Any veggies will work well...you just can't go wrong.

15-oz. can French-style green beans, drained
15-oz. can green peas, drained
15-oz. can whole kernel corn, drained
10-oz. jar pearl onions, cooked
1/4 c. butter
3 T. all-purpose flour
1 c. whipping cream
1/2 c. shredded Cheddar cheese
salt and pepper to taste
1 t. dry mustard
1/4 t. Worcestershire sauce
grated Parmesan cheese to taste

Combine vegetables in a lightly greased 13"x9" baking pan. Melt butter in a saucepan over medium heat; stir in flour. Cook together until well blended. Gradually stir in cream and continue stirring until sauce is thickened. Add cheese, salt, pepper, mustard and Worcestershire sauce. Stir until cheese is melted; pour over vegetables. Sprinkle with Parmesan cheese. Cover and bake at 350 degrees for 20 to 30 minutes. Serves 6 to 8.

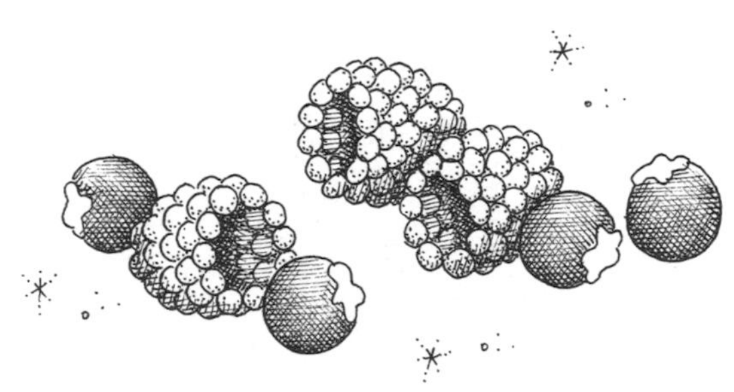

Serving gelatin for dessert? Give it some pizazz! Add fresh blueberries to lemon gelatin or stir in fresh raspberries with lime gelatin...so refreshing.

Creamed Spinach Casserole

Leah Finks
Gooseberry Patch

Only 4 ingredients...a breeze to make!

2 10-oz. pkgs. frozen chopped spinach, thawed and drained
8-oz. pkg. cream cheese, softened
1/4 c. milk
salt and pepper to taste
1/3 c. seasoned croutons, crushed

Mix together all ingredients except croutons. Spoon mixture into an ungreased one-quart casserole dish. Sprinkle with croutons. Bake at 350 degrees for 25 to 30 minutes, or until heated through. Serves 6.

Try this creamy, low-calorie salad dressing for any tossed side salad. Combine 1/2 cup non-fat yogurt, one cup fresh herbs and one to 2 tablespoons fresh lemon, lime or orange juice in a blender; process until smooth. Delicious!

Nutty Noodle Bake

Shelley Turner
Boise, ID

Mmm...walnuts, garlic and fresh veggies.

- 3 T. olive oil
- 2/3 c. chopped walnuts
- 1 onion, thinly sliced
- 2 carrots, peeled and coarsely grated
- 1 bunch Swiss chard, chopped
- 1 clove garlic, minced
- 1/3 c. fresh parsley, minced
- 1/2 t. dried thyme
- 1/2 c. soy sauce
- 1 c. sour cream
- salt to taste
- 3 c. egg noodles, cooked
- 2 c. shredded Monterey Jack cheese

Heat oil in a large skillet over medium heat; sauté walnuts until lightly golden. Remove with slotted spoon and set aside; stir in onion and carrots. Sauté until onion is tender; remove from skillet. Add chard, garlic, parsley and thyme; sauté until chard is soft. Mix together soy sauce and sour cream; add to chard mixture along with walnuts. Sprinkle with salt to taste; set aside. Place noodles in a greased 2-quart casserole dish. Spoon vegetable mixture over top; sprinkle with cheese. Bake at 400 degrees for 15 minutes, or until cheese is bubbly. Serves 6.

A warm casserole and a cheery bouquet are sure pick-me-ups for a friend who is feeling under the weather.

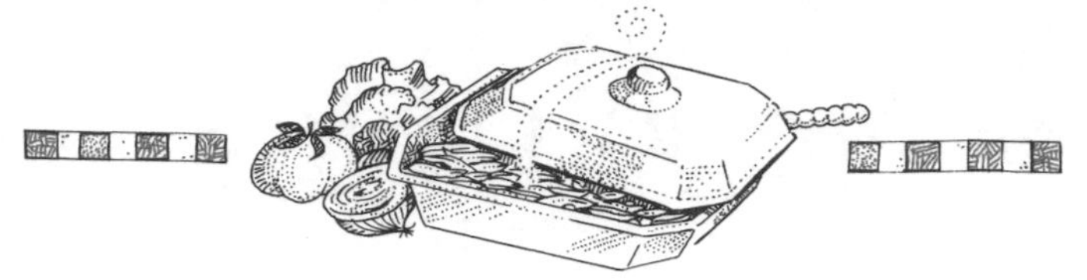

Country Baked Beans

Nancy Mershon
Whittier, CA

This homestyle recipe is a classic "must-have" any time, any place.

1 lb. bacon, diced
1 onion, chopped
56-oz. can pork & beans
1/4 c. molasses
1 T. vinegar
1/2 t. salt
1/4 c. brown sugar, packed
1/4 c. catsup
1/2 T. mustard

Cook bacon with onion until crisp; drain and crumble. Combine all ingredients in an ungreased 3-1/2 quart casserole dish. Bake, uncovered, at 300 degrees for 1-1/2 hours. Serves 10 to 12.

A molasses substitution in a pinch...an equal measurement of honey.

Black Bean Casserole

Tami Bowman
Gooseberry Patch

A no-fuss casserole...watch it disappear!

1/3 c. long-cooking brown rice, uncooked
1 c. vegetable broth
1 T. olive oil
1/3 c. onion, diced
1 zucchini, thinly sliced
1/2 c. sliced mushrooms
1/2 t. ground cumin
salt to taste
cayenne pepper to taste
15-oz. can black beans, drained and rinsed
4-oz. can diced green chiles, drained
1/3 c. carrots, peeled and shredded
2 c. shredded Swiss cheese, divided

Combine rice and vegetable broth in a saucepan and bring to a boil. Reduce heat to low; cover and simmer for 45 minutes. Set aside. Heat oil in a skillet over medium heat; sauté onion until tender. Stir in zucchini, mushrooms, cumin, salt and cayenne pepper. Cook and stir until zucchini is lightly golden. In a large bowl, mix rice, onion mixture, beans, chiles, carrots and one cup cheese. Pour into a greased 13"x9" baking pan; sprinkle with remaining cheese. Cover casserole loosely with aluminum foil. Bake at 350 degrees for 30 minutes. Uncover and continue baking 10 minutes, or until bubbly and lightly golden. Serves 6 to 8.

If you need to reheat rice to add to a casserole recipe, simply steam it in a colander over a pot of boiling water.

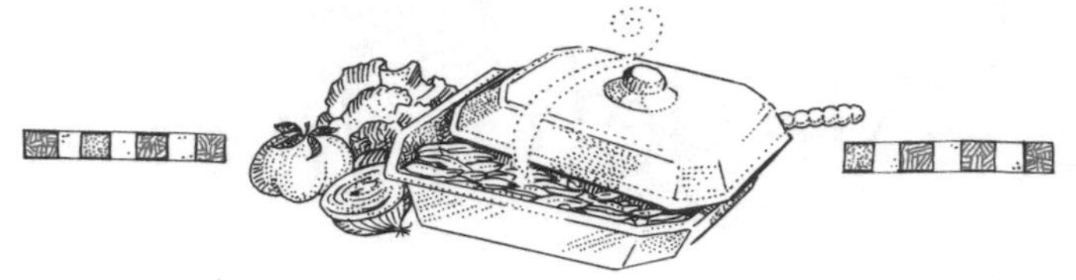

Pecan-Topped Sweet Potato Bake

Mary Coglianese
Kailua, HI

Garnish each serving with a pecan half for a pretty presentation.

3 c. sweet potatoes, boiled, peeled and mashed
1/2 c. sugar
1/2 c. butter
2 eggs, beaten
1 t. vanilla extract
1/3 c. milk

Combine all ingredients; mix until very smooth and spread in a lightly greased 11"x7" baking pan. Sprinkle topping over potato mixture and bake for 25 minutes at 350 degrees. Serve hot. Makes 4 to 6 servings.

Topping:

1/3 c. butter, melted
1 c. brown sugar, packed
1/2 c. all-purpose flour
1 c. chopped pecans

Combine all ingredients in a bowl; mix well.

A sweet & simple glow…set a votive candle inside a canning jar filled with coarse salt or rosehips. Line up several along a walkway or on porch steps.

Summery Herbed Tomato Pie

Janice O'Brien
Warrenton, VA

Refrigerated pie crust makes this one quick-to-fix meal.

9-inch pie crust
3 to 4 tomatoes, sliced
1/2 c. fresh chives, chopped
2 T. fresh basil, chopped
salt and pepper to taste
2 c. shredded mozzarella cheese
1/2 c. mayonnaise

Press pie crust into a 9" pie plate. Bake at 425 degrees for 5 minutes. Reduce oven to 400 degrees. Arrange tomato slices in crust; sprinkle with chives, basil, salt and pepper. Combine cheese and mayonnaise; spread over tomatoes. Bake at 400 degrees for 35 minutes.
Serves 8 to 10.

New terra cotta pots make terrific serving dishes for tall veggies like celery and carrots, or even silverware and plastic straws.

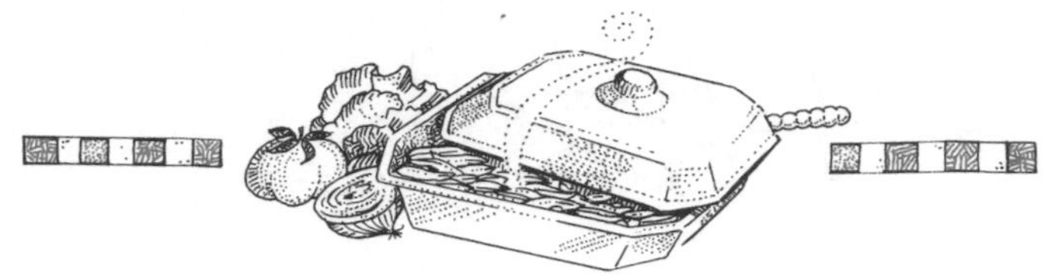

Quick & Easy Parmesan Asparagus

Paula Smith
Ottawa, IL

From oven to table in only 15 minutes!

4 lbs. asparagus, trimmed
1/4 c. butter, melted
2 c. shredded Parmesan cheese
1 t. salt
1/2 t. pepper

In a large skillet, add asparagus and one inch of water. Bring to a boil. Reduce heat; cover and simmer for 5 to 7 minutes, until crisp-tender. Drain and arrange asparagus in a greased 13"x9" baking pan. Drizzle with butter; sprinkle with Parmesan cheese, salt and pepper. Bake uncovered at 350 degrees for 10 to 15 minutes, or until cheese is melted. Serves 8 to 10.

A speedy way to crush tomatoes for any recipe…just cut tomatoes in half and rub the cut side against a grater.

Classic Green Bean Casserole

Reggie Westhoff
Monticello, MO

This is one of those all-time favorite recipes no kitchen should be without.

- 4 14-1/2 oz. cans green beans, drained
- 2 10-3/4 oz. cans cream of mushroom soup
- 1/3 c. milk
- 6-oz. can French fried onions

Mix beans, soup and milk together; spoon into an ungreased 13"x9" baking pan. Sprinkle with onions; bake at 350 degrees for 45 minutes. Serves 8 to 10.

Tasty casserole dishes are ideal for a new mom. Make several and deliver them to her before the baby arrives. She can freeze them now, then simply pop dinner in the oven to bake while baby naps.

Quick-Fix Casseroles

	Cooked Meat 2 c.	Starch 1 c.	Cooked Veggies 1 c.	Onion 1/2 c.	Sauce 1-1/2 c.	Seasoning 2 t.	Toppings
Breakfast & Brunch	sausage	potatoes, diced	green pepper, chopped	onion, chopped	cheese sauce	dried oregano	biscuit dough
Poultry	chicken	noodles, cooked	peas	green onion, sliced	tomato sauce	dried basil	crushed crackers
Seafood	shrimp	rice, cooked	carrots, diced	1 T. shallots, chopped	white sauce	dried parsley	crushed potato chips
Beef	beef	orzo, cooked	celery, chopped	1/2 t. onion powder	gravy	dried thyme	bread crumbs
Pork	pork	pasta shells, cooked	zucchini	pearl onions	cream soup	dried sage	grated cheese

To whip up a homestyle casserole in a flash, blend together the items in each row and place in a 2-quart casserole dish. Bake, covered, at 350 degrees for 30 minutes. Makes 4 servings.

Casserole & Baking Pan Match-Up

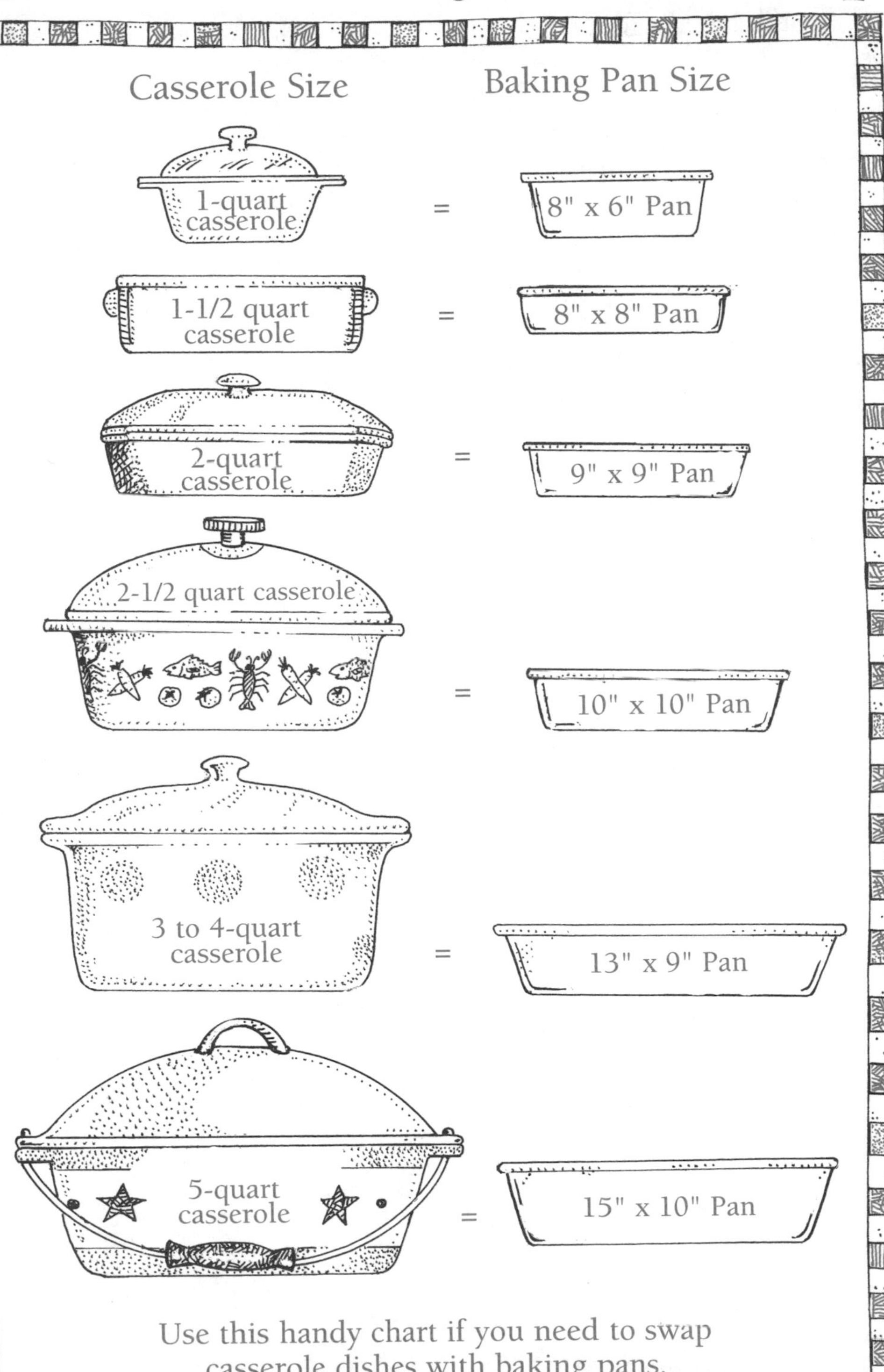

Basic Casserole List for Pantry and Refrigerator
all-purpose flour
onions
potatoes
frozen veggies
tomatoes
canned beans
tomato sauce
tomato paste
broth
canned cream soups
dried pasta
bread crumbs
rice
cheese
sour cream
mayonnaise
butter or margarine
oil
garlic
canned tuna
dried beans
canned fruit
nuts
SALT
Pepper
milk
carrots
catsup
mustard
refrigerated biscuits
mushrooms
eggs
poultry
beef
fish

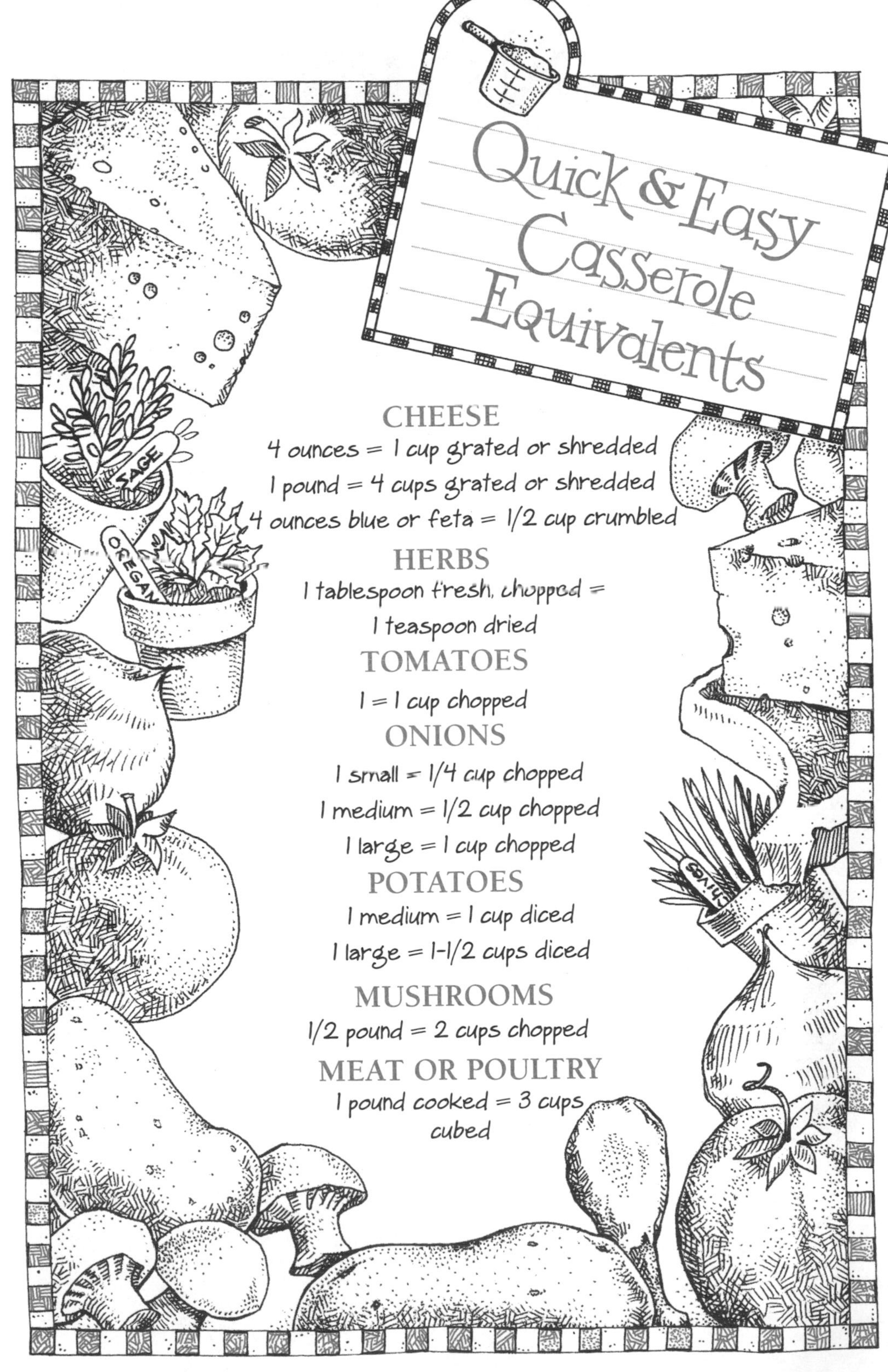

Quick & Easy Casserole Equivalents

CHEESE

4 ounces = 1 cup grated or shredded

1 pound = 4 cups grated or shredded

4 ounces blue or feta = 1/2 cup crumbled

HERBS

1 tablespoon fresh, chopped =
1 teaspoon dried

TOMATOES

1 = 1 cup chopped

ONIONS

1 small = 1/4 cup chopped

1 medium = 1/2 cup chopped

1 large = 1 cup chopped

POTATOES

1 medium = 1 cup diced

1 large = 1-1/2 cups diced

MUSHROOMS

1/2 pound = 2 cups chopped

MEAT OR POULTRY

1 pound cooked = 3 cups
cubed

INDEX

Beef

Breakfast & Brunch

Pork

INDEX

Poultry

Seafood

INDEX

Vegetable

all-American just like Mom's hearty

satisfying

homestyle

tried & true good food homecooked laughter old-fashioned

U.S. to Canadian recipe equivalents

Volume Measurements

1/4 teaspoon	1 mL
1/2 teaspoon	2 mL
1 teaspoon	5 mL
1 tablespoon = 3 teaspoons	15 mL
2 tablespoons = 1 fluid ounce	30 mL
1/4 cup	60 mL
1/3 cup	75 mL
1/2 cup = 4 fluid ounces	125 mL
1 cup = 8 fluid ounces	250 mL
2 cups = 1 pint =16 fluid ounces	500 mL
4 cups = 1 quart	1 L

Weights

1 ounce	30 g
4 ounces	120 g
8 ounces	225 g
16 ounces = 1 pound	450 g

Oven Temperatures

300° F	150° C
325° F	160° C
350° F	180° C
375° F	190° C
400° F	200° C
450° F	230° C

Baking Pan Sizes

Square

8x8x2 inches	2 L = 20x20x5 cm
9x9x2 inches	2.5 L = 23x23x5 cm

Rectangular

13x9x2 inches	3.5 L = 33x23x5 cm

Loaf

9x5x3 inches	2 L = 23x13x7 cm

Round

8x1-1/2 inches	1.2 L = 20x4 cm
9x1-1/2 inches	1.5 L = 23x4 cm